MW00913040

# Return on Investment? or Reliability of Income?

THE TRUE MEANING OF "ROI"
IN THE GOLDEN YEARS...

## Alan Becker

Retirement Solutions Group, Inc.
Overland Park, Kansas

Alan Becker/Retirement Solutions Group, Inc.
6801 W. 107th St.
Overland Park, KS 66212
www.rsgusa.net

Book layout ©2013 BookDesignTemplates.com

Ordering information:
For details, contact the address above.

Return on Investment? or Reliability of Income? / Alan Becker —1st ed.
ISBN 978-1523763504

# Contents

*This book is dedicated to all those who seek the knowledge and have the strength to implement what they learn for a better tomorrow for themselves and the ones they love. For my grandparents, who have gone before me and have left a legacy of knowledge to follow; and my parents, who raised me the best they could, teaching me values and morals that I can pass on to my sons.*

# Preface

When it comes to retirement planning, we are given a lot of information that could be considered conflicting. At the end of the day, we are often left trying to sift through and figure out what is the truth. I think truth may be a relative term, unfortunately. We are brought up in society to conform to a way of thinking that should allow us to function in and help us to be productive members of said society. We will then form social relationships and friendships based on further deciding who best fits into our ethical beliefs and moral standards. This thought can be applied to many facets of life including our careers, social lives and relationships — YOU NAME IT! Birds of a feather flock together, so to speak.

The purpose of this book is to get you looking at your life from the retirement planning perspective. Some people avoid doing so, and this can be detrimental to one's financial future to and through the journey we call retirement. I also ask, as you read further, to take into account that I am writing this book from the view of an entrepreneur, or in other words, as a risk-taker. For many, this is uncomfortable; however, it is required for progress when dictating one's own retirement. Without individuals to stand out and try something new or show you another perspective, we wouldn't have forward momentum or concept advancement. Step out of the box and let me grab your eyes, ears and thoughts. If all you ever do is listen to those immediately around you, something bigger may be missed by not being open-minded and exploring new theories and possibilities.

Alan with mentor/friend/entrepreneur/author Darren Hardy.

Darren Hardy, an entrepreneur, mentor and friend, has written books and interviewed many of the great minds of our times from his position as the publisher of SUCCESS Magazine. I have had the pleasure of spending a few days with Darren to learn and understand his theories and business principles. He tells the story of an eagle's egg falling from a tree. Once the egg lands, it rolls down a hill to a farm where a group of chickens finds it and raises it as their own. The eagle spends its days living life as a chicken. He frequently looks up at the sky above, watching the eagles soar in the sky, thinking how wonderful it would be to fly like they did. Unfortunately for the eagle, he was continually told by his adoptive flock that he was just a chicken and that he couldn't fly with the eagles as he so yearned. So, the eagle lived by others' beliefs, not knowing that under-

neath it all, he had every ability to soar as he so desired. He didn't stay grounded due to ability; he stayed grounded due to not exploring his own thoughts, ideas and abilities himself.

How does this all apply? Let me see if I can help make sense of this for you. For starters, I want to be very clear that I am NOT anti-market. Society tells us to use the stock market, and this is not good or bad, it just simply "is." There are several reasons for this and Wall Street does have the ability to be a wonderful thing; however, I feel it has a specific time and a place. The media, whether print or digital, is controlled by Wall Street. The television stations spend more of their resources telling us of tragedy and doom and gloom because that is what sells. These same media sources have stockholders and political commentary, and the programming on a network is based on that network's viewer demographics. Being a business owner for the last 18 years has been eye opening, to put it lightly, yet I wouldn't have had it any other way. One thing you learn quickly, though, is that anything you want is a matter of the almighty dollar.

People often ask me why everyone isn't using insurance in their planning portfolio or using the concept of our ideas in their planning repertoire. The insurance side of the financial planning business comprises agents and their abilities to foster relationships with both prospective and current clients. This has been true since the time of the door-to-door insurance salesman who came by every week to collect the premiums. Today, not a lot has changed as it is still very much a relationship-based business. We don't have control of mainstream media, and there isn't enough money based on regulations and volume for the insurance carriers to compete on the same level as the stock market. The goal of most every company is to go public and have the private investor invest in them in the form of stock. You can't flip through the television channels, look at a newspaper or surf the Web without seeing the latest stock market indexes.

Insurance and the stock market are two different vehicles that have different elements of risk. Both systems have places they fit best in a plan, and you as an individual and a consumer should know your options, EVERY ONE OF THEM. You should decide for yourself what makes the most sense for you and your loved ones. Creating your own paycheck in retirement is foundational and should be done with guarantees. Growth can be done through the market if you understand the potential for the roller coaster it can be. Positioned correctly, you can use both industries together. It's like going to the hospital and talking to an MD and a surgeon — the surgeon may be quick to the operating room because that's what he knows and feels comfortable with, but does that mean a less invasive procedure couldn't create the same outcome?

If you can achieve your goals without unnecessary risk while getting exactly what you want, is this not achievement of the goal? My clients realize that they have worked their entire lives for what they currently hold as assets, and the "finish line" is quickly approaching. You have many choices, and you need to be comfortable with those choices. We have found that great increases of wealth later in life has very little effect on people as their values, ethics and beliefs have already been established.

When the Titanic set sail, the captain was told by the manufacturer that the ship was unsinkable. Yet we all know that it sank. Who do you blame? The captain? The manufacturer? I conclude it was the captain; he had seven different warnings and chose to ignore them all. In retirement, you are the captain of your own ship, and if the market leaves you sinking, you have no one to blame but yourself — not your advisor, for you are the captain of your own ship. Most of us don't have the luxury of a do-over.

At Retirement Solutions Group, Inc., I have built a philosophy around honest communication and using the correct product for the job. Your goals and needs dictate the product, not the other way around. When you hear the word "retirement," what pops into your mind? I do a lot of public speaking on the subject from a financial point of view, and I am always intrigued at the answers I get when I pose that question to a group of people. Everyone seems to have a different vision. What's yours?

According to the Merriam-Webster dictionary, the word "retire" means "to withdraw." That definition doesn't seem to fit the active generation of today's retirees. The word on the street these days is that 60 is the new 40, 70 is the new 50 and so on. People are healthier and living longer. Those approaching retirement have an entirely different view of retirement than their parents. Instead of rocking on the front porch, today's retiree is more apt to pick up a guitar and start a rock band!

Living longer can be a good thing. Today, the average age of someone moving into a nursing home is 81. In the 1950s, it was 65. In a 2005 Merrill Lynch survey of people between the ages of 40 and 59, some 76 percent said they planned to retire when they were about 64 — and then start an entirely new career. When happy with existing careers, many folks wonder, "Why should I retire?" For some, retirement is time to finally do what they have always wanted to do, not what they had to do to raise a family. Second careers among senior citizens have become more and more commonplace. Have you seen how many men and women in their 70s and 80s are participating in marathons? In the classroom today, you are apt to see seniors taking classes and teaching them as well. Retirement, instead of closing a door on active life, opens a door to fuller lives for more and more Americans.

There are impacts and considerations to make with these changes in the picture of what retirement encompasses. For instance, in the 1950s, life expectancy was 62, and full retirement age was 65. Now full retirement age is 66, but many people live into their 80s, 90s and even past 100. For active seniors starting new careers, when to take Social Security and taxation issues from receiving Social Security and income wages are important considerations in their plans.

As a retirement planner, it is my job to keep up with all of the latest news on the financial side of retirement. I get approximately 30 magazines and brochures each month containing articles examining one facet or another of this phase of our economic lives. The artwork that goes with the articles always shows a happy, silver-haired couple laughing, smiling and either holding hands strolling down the beach or playing in a sunlit field with their grandchildren. They don't seem to have a care in the world. Are those pictures real life? NO, they're not! Retirement in real life is a crossroads of concerns for many. Have I saved enough money? Will I outlive my assets and end up being a burden on my loved ones? Are my assets safe? Do I have them properly invested? What happens if I get sick? Am I properly insured? Is Social Security threatened?

One thing is certain: We will only be able to fulfill our retirement dreams if the assets necessary to do so actually exist. Is the concern that the wealth we have worked so hard to accumulate is eroding? Yes. If you don't believe that, just ask some of the folks who lost a sizable chunk of their life savings in the last stock market crash because of poor planning. Or interview someone who labored under the delusion that property values could never decrease and sunk all of their assets into real estate prior to the bursting of the last housing bubble in 2007.

To be truly happy in retirement, you must be financially secure. Worrying about what is going on up or down on Wall Street doesn't seem to fit that puzzle, and neither does fretting over whether you will have enough money left at the end of the month to pay bills. A truly happy and financially secure retirement means that you are confident about the future, not hunkered over your computer watching the ticker symbols bob up and down or glued to your TV straining to hear the next predictions made by the talking heads on CNBC. You may be one of those people who enjoys trading in the stock market — just for the fun of it. If you are, that's fine, but there does come a time when a DIY approach is too risky and it is time to turn over the reins to a qualified and experienced professional.

It is one thing to have a job after retirement because you want to work. It is quite another to have a job after you retire doing something you don't really want to do, because you HAVE to work. I know of one man who is 75 and owns an automobile dealership and a real estate firm. He could have retired years ago, but he loves his work. He would be in agony on a golf course or strolling on a beach. His idea of recreation is to hang around the dealership or show a home to a prospective buyer.

## How Do I Enter Retirement Without the Worries?

My primary focus when I wrote this book was to give you the information you need to set yourself up with income for life without ever having to work again in retirement. But there is no easy fix or silver bullet. There is no one-size-fits-all. I cannot tell you how many people I have sat across the table from in one of the conference rooms of Retirement Solutions Group, Inc., who had been "sold" a "retirement product" instead of having a true retirement plan devised and implemented. No two individuals are alike. Even the term "identical twins" is a bit of a misnomer; they may have identical DNA but they have different fingerprints. So it stands to reason that no two financial plans should be identical. Take two individuals who are the same age, work for the same company, have the same size family, live across the street from each other in identical houses, earn the same annual salary and have the same amount of money in the bank — they will still need individual financial planning. Why? Because their values are different! Their goals are different! Money, after all, is only paper, coins or numbers on an account statement if there is no purpose attached to it. What do you want your money to do for you? That's the key question.

The approach you take to your retirement will be uniquely yours. What are your dreams? What are your goals? What do you want your money to do for you? Yogi Berra, who is famous for his malapropisms, is quoted as saying: "You have to be careful if you don't know where you're going; you might not end up there." I am often asked how much a person should have in reserve before he or she can comfortably retire. That's a bit of a loaded question, isn't it? The answer is, "It depends." It depends on a number of things that are unique to you.

## Keep an Open Mind

In this book, we will cover many retirement strategies. Some of these strategies may be familiar to you, and some may be new. I urge you to approach the information you see presented with an open mind. Many of the ideas and concepts we will discuss in the pages of this book may challenge what you have always thought to be true. A teacher once asked me: "If something you thought was true turned out to be false, when would you want to know?" If you do run across an unfamiliar concept, I invite you to resist the human tendency to cling to an idea just because it is comfortable. The retirement landscape is changing and we are on a journey, just as old maps don't work on new highways. At one time, seat belts were "those newfangled straps" that got in the way. Nowadays you wouldn't think of driving a car without them. Until Roth IRAs and 401(k)s came along, no one had ever heard of them, either. Now they are part of our retirement vocabulary. At some point, everything was new.

Please also know that my objective is to educate and inform. The views expressed here are not just mine, but those of many who have helped do the research for this project. When it comes to your financial future, you are the ultimate decision-maker.

So however you came to read my book, I appreciate your attention. I know your time is valuable. When you listen to a philosophy such as mine and find that it's outside the box a bit, I ask you, "Is it really?" Perhaps it is just being censored, and perhaps we have found an outlet to get you the information that works — just without all the noise!

# CHAPTER 1

# The Three Stages of Money

Curious, I stuck my head inside the office of a Navy recruiting office in Kansas City at the age of 17, fresh out of high school. I told the man in the crisp white uniform that I wanted to go to college. "We got college," he said. I scored high on the entrance test and thus qualified for the Navy College Fund. This was incredibly important to me because I didn't want to burden my parents with paying for college, nor did I want to burden myself with student loans. Since I was only 17, my father had to sign for me and I had to enter the DEP (Delayed Entry Program) to enlist. I think that day I came home and told my parents that I intended to join the Navy was the proudest day of their lives.

My first assignment after hitting the fleet was cleaning berths as a ship's serviceman aboard the USS Ranger CV-61 sailing out of San Diego, California. I soon found my Navy "calling" when they taught me how to cut hair. As a barber aboard this giant floating city, I would learn much more about life than I could have ever imagined. I also learned about the sea, having traversed hundreds of thousands of miles before my four-year tour of duty ended (two years on USS Ranger CV-61 and two years on DD976 – USS Merrill). One thing I learned about the sea is that it is unpredictable. One day the sky can be as blue as a robin's egg and the water as smooth as mirrored glass. The next day, it can be an angry gray tempest producing giant waves that can rattle the largest ships in the ocean — even an aircraft carrier weighing 56,000 tons where I lived and worked.

A teenaged sailor and his proud mother, Fran.

The ups and downs of the stock market are like the crests and troughs of the sea on an ocean crossing. When you are on the open water, you get used to the rhythmic rise and fall of ocean swells. The stock market can resemble this too, rising and falling in steady rhythm and undulation, like the breathing of a slumbering beast, only to awaken without warning and produce a tempest that can threaten the world with economic collapse. When I was first stationed on the old lady, I was excited yet scared at the same time. However, once I became accustomed to her, I was comfortable even though I wasn't in control of the destination but fully open to the journey. Sound familiar? It reminds me of a retiree entering the realm of retirement.

When Hurricane Sandy roared up the Atlantic seaboard in the fall of 2012, one of the casualties was a 50-year-old replica of the 18th century HMS Bounty, which had been built for use in filming "Mutiny on the Bounty," the one starring Marlon Brando in the role of the mutineer, Fletcher Christian. The three-masted schooner went down 90 miles east of Cape Hatteras, North Carolina, as giant 30-foot waves, kicked up by the storm, would later ravish the shorelines of New York and New Jersey, causing billions of dollars in damage.

It was not just the rough seas that did in the old schooner, as she had survived heavier seas than that. It was the combination of the high waves and the failure of the ship's diesel engines that did her in. Fourteen members of the crew were saved, one drowned, and the captain was never found. In the U.S. Coast Guard hearings that followed, it was determined that Captain Robin Walbridge, the skipper of the vessel, had made poor decisions and should have sought safety in a nearby port. It was his responsibility to evaluate the risks versus the rewards for each possible course of action, including seeking shelter from the storm. Most likely, he paid the ultimate price and lost his life to the sea, along with one of his crew.

As with the sea, when it comes to managing our money, there are varying degrees of risk and danger. Protection from economic storms often comes in understanding those risks and recognizing the dangers. If you were a crew member of a sailing ship, you would appreciate having a captain who possessed not only experience, but also one with the wisdom not to take inordinate risks. Now, granted, this is an imperfect analogy — of course unlike a crew member, you are the one who is ultimately in control of your proverbial ship. But it's likely — and prudent — that you will look to a financial advisor for guidance. Prior to the last great stock market crash, many advisors were lulled into complacency, reasoning perhaps that they have traversed these seas before without incident. Why should now be different? But different it was. They had forgotten lesson No. 1 in dealing with other people's money: **It's not what you make on the upside, but what you keep on the downside that counts.**

Warren Buffett, the "Oracle of Omaha," third-richest person in the world in 2013, worth $54 billion, give or take a million or two, and one of the most respected investors on the planet, says there are two rules of investing:

- Rule No. 1 is *never lose money.*
- Rule No. 2 is *never forget rule No. 1!*

# Three Stages of Wealth

The three stages of wealth are:

- Accumulation
- Preservation
- Distribution

When you are young, you are in the **accumulation stage.** You finish your education, you get married (or not), you start a family (or not), you get a job (in order to be a contributing member of society, one is almost always required), you collect your paychecks and, if you are smart, you try to put away a healthy amount each pay period into a savings program. These days, with pensions becoming extinct, it is probably a defined contribution plan like a 401(k), or some other tax-deferred retirement plan.

If you don't have a "paycheck job" — let's say you are in business for yourself — then you may have your own retirement savings account, perhaps an individual retirement account (IRA). In any case, during the accumulation stage, you have time on your side. Common advice suggests you can make it work for you by steadily, every week or every month, pumping money into your plan like a little oil well so that it has the potential to grow until you retire.

The key here is to save *regularly* and *consistently* and don't touch it. Maintain an emergency fund of about three to six months' income set aside in cash, or something else extremely liquid, so you won't be tempted to tap your reserves in case some unexpected expense pops up. Let's face it, life happens, and you could be confronted by a sudden illness, the loss of employment or even a natural disaster. Many things could happen that could cause your savings plan to derail. Without an emergency fund, you may be tempted to put savings on the back burner.

Each pay period, most of you have the opportunity to contribute to your employer-sponsored retirement (defined contribution) plan. Hopefully, your employer will match your contribution. If that is the case, regardless of the percentage of the match, please consider taking advantage of this. It's free money. Of course, it's a tax deduction for your employer to do this, but some employers are more generous than others in this regard. Additionally, it may be in your best interest to see what else is available rather than your 401(k) once you have met the match. You don't need to add risk where it's not necessary. I believe there are other strategies to utilize funds beyond the employer match. So after you take advantage of the free money at work, you may want to consider allocating a portion of your retirement savings to more conservative vehicles, such as products that lock in your gains each year and provide principal protection.

Mixing conservative assets into your portfolio can help you avoid having to play catch up if a significant market correction affects your investments. On a side note, if you have a 401(k) at an old job, you will need to decide whether to leave it where it is or roll it over and take it with you. Working with an independent financial advisor can help you figure out which option works better for you.

Sometimes I see clients who have all but forgotten about some of their assets because they left them with former employers, so I stress the importance of keeping track of what you have and where you have it. Additionally, working with a financial advisor can help you avoid having too many of your retirement resources in one area. Enron should have taught us that too much of your retirement savings shouldn't be in one company's stock, even if you work there.

During your working years, you are the beneficiary of something called "dollar cost averaging." Take a 401(k), for example. Let's say that $100 per week of your paycheck goes into your 401(k). Typically, the 401(k) custodian uses that money to buy shares in mutual funds. You likely have an opportunity once a year or so to decide in general terms how you wish to have that money invested according to your risk tolerance.

Dollar cost averaging is on your side when you are young: when the market is up, your share value is up; when the market is down, your $100 just bought more shares. While this won't protect you from market volatility, those skinny shares will fatten up when the market rebounds. While your stock values will still be subject to volatility, by consistently contributing in both up and down markets, in some ways you can put that volatility to work on your behalf by ultimately lowering your overall cost per share.

When you are young, you should be able to afford some of these risks; however, I recommend you build foundationally. You wouldn't build a house from the roof down; you build from the foundation up. For several reasons, the roof is the most vulnerable to the elements. There are three common ways to build a foundation: a crawl space, a basement or a slab. Which one would you recommend?

This is a trick question, because it would depend on your location and your age or health. A basement in the Midwest, where I am from, is preferable if you can navigate the stairs, in part because of the extra space but especially because of their resiliency and protection during tornado season. However, if you lived at lower sea level, your basement would be an indoor swimming pool. As in this example, there are different viable solutions to different scenarios, just as with investing. I believe you need to establish some fundamental baselines to help protect a portion of your assets from market volatility and give you some level of assurance that you won't run out of money in retirement.

## The Time Value of Money

Money has both an intrinsic value and a time value. The intrinsic value is obvious — a dollar buys a candy bar. The time value of money, or TVM, is more difficult to wrap our minds around. If more young people knew and understood TVM, we would see more 40-year-old millionaires. TVM is the value of money figuring in a given amount of interest earned.

For example, $100 of today's money invested for one year and earning 5 percent interest will be worth $105 after one year. Oh yeah? Big deal, right? But let's say you started with that same $100 and added just $10 per month to it, and it grew at 5 percent interest compounded annually for 30 years. How much would you have? **$8,404.86**. That will send you on a nice vacation, right? If you are young, just think of how many dollars and cents you waste in a month.

Just for grins, consider this example. Get a job, save up $1,000. Now, put that $1,000 to work at 5 percent interest compounded annually for 30 years and add $100 every month. In 30 years, you have $84,048. Let it grow for another 10 years, and you'll have almost double that! Did I catch your attention yet?

# How Much Is a Penny Worth?

Compounding interest is mostly a matter of time. To give you some perspective, let's say, hypothetically, Christopher Columbus wades ashore in the New World back in 1492 and finds a penny. He puts it in his pocket, and when he returns to Spain he puts it in the bank at 6 percent compounding interest.

Take a guess at how much the penny would be worth today.

Would you believe over $120 billion?

I know you have heard the story about how Manhattan was sold by Native Americans to the Dutch for $24 worth of beads and trinkets in 1626. At first, it sounds like the Dutch got some of the most expensive real estate in the world at a real steal, doesn't it? Yet a mathematician once figured out that if the Manhattoes tribe, which sold the island they called "Manna-Hattin," had invested the proceeds of the sale in a bank, with 6 percent interest compounded annually for close to 400 years, they would have over $175,000,000,000 ($175 billion) today — that's the power of compound interest!

Clearly these examples are extreme and unrealistic, but is it any wonder that Albert Einstein called compound interest the eighth wonder of the modern world?

A few years ago, I was speaking before a group of young people about investing at least something for the long term, even if your resources are limited. Just to make the point that persistent saving pays off, even with small amounts, I asked them a question: If you had to choose between (a) $1 million or (b) a penny doubled every day for 30 days, which would you choose?

Nearly every hand went up for the million dollars. The ones who opted for the doubling penny must have known that it was a trick question.

The penny doubling every day for 30 days would end up being $5,368,709.12!

Following is the proof:

| | | DAY | AMOUNT | DAY | AMOUNT |
|---|---|---|---|---|---|
| | | 1 | $.01 | 16 | $327.68 |
| | | 2 | $.02 | 17 | $655.36 |
| | | 3 | $.04 | 18 | $1,310.12 |
| WHAT DO YOU | | 4 | $.08 | 19 | $2,621.44 |
| GET IF YOU | | 5 | $.16 | 20 | $5,242.88 |
| DOUBLE A PENNY | | 6 | $.32 | 21 | $10,485.76 |
| EVERY DAY FOR | | 7 | $.64 | 22 | $20,971.52 |
| 30 DAYS? | | 8 | $1.28 | 23 | $41,943.04 |
| | | 9 | $2.56 | 24 | $83,866.06 |
| $5,368,709.12 | | 10 | $5.12 | 25 | $167,772.16 |
| | | 11 | $10.24 | 26 | $335,544.32 |
| | | 12 | $20.48 | 27 | $671,088.64 |
| | | 13 | $40.96 | 28 | $1,342,177.28 |
| | | 14 | $81.92 | 29 | $2,684,354.56 |
| | | 15 | $163.84 | 30 | $5,368,709.12 |

The "doubling penny" illustrates the time value of money and the principle of patience in savings and investing. Slow and steady wins the race most every time. Notice how the real payoff happens toward the end of the 30 days? It's like a snowball rolling downhill; the longer it rolls, the bigger it gets. Money growing at compound interest is the same phenomenon; a small amount put aside and allowed to grow with the interest compounded can amount to a tidy sum.

Now, most financial vehicles don't work exactly like this: between market volatility, unpredictable returns and account fees, nothing is ever so straightforward. However, I wanted to illustrate what a powerful tool *time* can be when it's on your side, and when you have the space to allow a financial product to take advantage of compounding interest at whatever rate.

## Preservation Stage

All good things come to an end, and so does the accumulation stage of our economic lives. But when? It is not necessarily when we are finished accumulating. We hope, unless someone pulls the plug on the concept of investing, our money will continue working for us on through our retirement years and we will be able to pass it on to the next generation. Our mindsets typically change from an accumulation focus to a preservation focus when we reach the point of retirement, and maybe even a few years before. Why? Because we can no longer take the same risks with our money in those years that we did when we were younger.

My favorite analogy for this is the end zone in the game of football. One principle of playing football is that when you are in the "red zone," or 20 yards from the goal line, you must protect the ball. It is no time to play fast and loose with the "rock," as they call that precious oblate spheroid tucked securely under the arm of the quarterback or running back. Fumble here and you blow it big time. That's why simple, conservative plays are usually called in the huddle when you are within 20 yards of the goal.

Retirement is the goal line. If you are five years away from it, you must be careful that you don't "lose the rock." It's easy to do if you make risky decisions. You no longer have time on your side as you did 20 years ago. Historically, stock markets recover from crashes, but not necessarily right away. The nation took years recovering from the crash of 2008. Some recoveries are quicker than others, such as in the case of the 1987 crash; it took the economy only two years for the Dow to get back to where it once was. The recovery from the 1929 crash was more difficult, spanning more than a quarter century. Young investors can usually ride that roller coaster. Those approaching retirement can't afford to take the chance, especially if they will need those funds to see them through their retirement.

Now see why this "red zone," or five years before retirement, is called the "preservation stage" of our economic lives? If 2008 happened today, the economic effect on retirees would be more widespread as, by some estimates, 10,000 baby boomers per day are aging into retirement and beginning to draw or move their retirement funds, meaning that the portion of our overall population in the retired demographic is rapidly increasing.

## Distribution Stage

The last economic phase is the ***distribution stage.*** This is where we say goodbye to our jobs and begin collecting our Social Security and tapping our savings to replace our paychecks. Defined benefit pension plans, once popular with large employers, are drying up. Replacing them are defined contribution retirement plans, such as 401(k)s. Yet in a way it isn't entirely your money. You will have to pay Uncle Sam his cut when you reach 70 ½. One difference between the two is that pensions are guaranteed to last the lifetime of the retiree, whereas defined contribution plans are not. Defined contribution plans, like any investment, may run out of funds **unless** you take steps to protect at least a portion of your assets from market risk. According to some surveys, the No. 1 fear among American retirees is running out of money. It's not just the money; it's the independence their assets represent. No one wants to become a burden on his or her family in retirement.

**Here's why:**

The reason dollar cost averaging (or reverse amortization) can help those in the accumulation stage is because they are constantly **adding** to the account. It could also hurt those in retirement because they are constantly **withdrawing** from the account. The cost of living during one's retirement will likely remain somewhat constant, which will require the constant withdrawal of a consistent amount to cover it. Whenever these withdrawals are made from a market-based account, such as a 401(k), shares are sold from the account in order to cut the check. Whether the market is up or down, the withdrawals continue. More shares are sold when the market is down and fewer shares are sold when the market is up, but the erosion of the account is accelerated by the downside withdrawals. This concept is called *reverse dollar cost averaging.*

Those who are approaching retirement simply must develop a personal retirement income strategy as a protection against the risks that are inherent with the paradigm shift (from saving to spending) they are making in their financial lives. You may ask, so what are the risks? Here are a few:

- **Longevity.** Your generation is living longer on average than any generation before it. Blame it on improved health care or cessation of smoking, your money will have to go farther if it is to last as long as you do. There is a 25 percent chance today that the husband or wife of a married couple age 65 will live to age 95. It's a good problem, but it presents a new set of circumstances to be dealt with.
- **Inflation.** Things look pretty tame as this book is being written but that could easily change. Over the course of your retirement, your an-

nual income needs could more than double. Just taking the relatively low inflation rate of 2.5 percent, if you need $50,000 per year to meet expenses in retirement now, you will need more than $90,000 for living expenses in 25 years to maintain the same standard of living. Imagine how that number would be affected if we should see a spike in the inflation rate such as the one experienced in the late 1970s and early 1980s.

- **Health care.** Health care can be one of the biggest expenses in retirement. A couple who retired at age 65 in 2010 may need $255,000 to cover health care expenses in retirement, according to one study by the Employee Benefit Research Institute. Retiring at age 65 in 2020, a couple may need $427,000 to cover the same expenses. Ouch! You must be properly educated on Medicare Supplements vs. Advantage plans, and you should talk with an agent who represents all the options.

- **Poor market performance.** We have already seen a good dose of this. Observers are calling the 2000s the "lost decade," and the "flat decade," because of the poor performance of the stock market. It wasn't that the market didn't move. It moved plenty. Thirty points up, then 30 points down, again and again, with even wilder swings at times. But in the end, if you flattened out the lines of the graph, there was no, or very little, progress. Maybe a 4 percent gain. Investors did not move exactly as the market moved — some did better, some worse — but most investors were affected in some way by the volatility.

*Unless you take steps to protect your assets,* you could be caught in the vice of having to depend on an asset that is subject to losses due to market reversals in your retirement. The thing you have to ask yourself is, (a) "Do I have the time to wait out another bear market?" and (b) "Do I have the resources to do so?"

Prior to retirement, it becomes time to move assets from the roof of our financial house to the foundation. We have to decide what the purpose of the money is. Our foundational monies now need to provide income, as well as continuing to grow or appreciate in value. Picture a house that you rent out. The purchase price of the house is $100,000, and the next year it is valued at

$105,000, which is a 5 percent return on investment. The following year, the value of the house slides down to $95,000 and your investment has lost value, a typical situation that many investors find themselves in when they rely on the stock market for asset growth. However, there is a second value to the rental house called the income, or yield that is generated from the monthly rent. Each month the owner collects rent, the funds are considered income or, the industry term, yield. For monies that are purposed to be retirement funds, it is equally as important to have yield (income) as it is to have appreciation. Just like the house, your retirement portfolio should be allocated both for growth and income.

Those are just a few reasons why it is important to develop a personal retirement income strategy as you shift gears into retirement. You are moving from saving money to managing the income from that savings. The challenge is to protect and defend what you have, make it grow and see to it that it cares for you the rest of your life. After you have your monthly bills taken care of, experience has taught me you better also have a guaranteed "playcheck." I would never want you to come home to mama and tell her we are doing without vacation or entertainment because the market has affected your retirement savings adversely. "Happy wife, happy life," right?

In retirement, we have three subcategories of the distribution phase of life:

- **Go-Go Years** — Every day is Saturday, the one day we spend the most money, so hopefully you're healthy, wealthy and wise enough to enter this stage early enough to enjoy it.
- **Slow-Go Years** — Getting a little worse for wear, it is getting more difficult to travel and lug the DPM (durable portable medical) equipment with you. You're getting tired and going to bed earlier.
- **No-Go Years** — Not sure this one needs much explanation. Traveling doesn't seem much fun. Health care costs become a larger concern.

The aforementioned phases are what you should prepare for, as no one knows how long they will last. Everyone's situation and health are different, so working with the right financial advisor can help you insure these transitions can be planned for and addressed proactively.

# CHAPTER 2

# Beware of the Hype

We live in a world flooded with information. In fact, the term "information overload" has been used to describe this peculiar ailment that afflicts our society today. You will also hear the phrases "information glut," "infobesity," "data smog" and "information explosion." Alvin Toffler, in his bestselling book, "Future Shock," discusses the difficulty people can have understanding an issue and making decisions; not because they don't have enough information but because they have too much. That book was published in 1970, by the way — far in advance of the Internet, email, smartphones and tablet-sized computers. Toffler predicted a world in which people would not be able to adjust to the quickening pace of society due to the advancement of technology. I believe that, on many levels, he was right.

There is a veritable tsunami of financial advice these days. Because people have unlimited access to so many tips, recommendations, guidance and expert opinions on how to manage their money, the result isn't clarity; conversely, it's confusion. It's a bit like playing on a basketball team with 15 coaches shouting out conflicting instructions as to what to do with the ball. Recently, I entered the words "financial advice" into the Google search bar and there were over 4 million responses.

I cannot believe how many magazines these days are devoted to finance. While perusing the shelves of a bookstore, I passed by the magazine section. Is it me, or has the number of magazines tripled in the last decade or so? The magazine section of this bookstore occupied one entire wall of the store. There were magazines for just about every vocation and avocation under the sun — everything from hot rods to dog grooming. Naturally, my eyes drifted to the financial section. Once again, I was amazed! Magazines on money and finance covered one entire 12-foot-wide section of the wall. The old standbys were there: Barron's, SmartMoney and Kiplinger's. But there were several others that I had never heard of, all of them competing for attention with blaring, sensational headlines like:

- **Buy as Much Gold as You Can Get Your Hands On**
- **Grab These Bonds for 10% Yields**

And my personal favorite:

- **RUN FOR THE HILLS!** *Top Financial Adviser Sees Imminent Collapse of U.S. Civilization!*

Those were actual magazine headlines. I realize that these personal finance magazines have to attract readers to buy their issues off the crowded rack, but I have a problem with some of the content found in the pages of these periodicals.

Impressionable readers who buy the magazines and actually make investment decisions based on what they read can lose big-time. Search all you want through each of these magazines, but you won't find an address to write to and get a refund if your investment doesn't pan out. Even some of the older, more conservative financial magazines have grown more sensational on their front pages. Here are some headlines that graced some of their front pages:

- ➢ **Stocks That Pay 8%** (Kiplinger's Personal Finance)
- ➢ **How to Get 8% on Your Money** (SmartMoney)
- ➢ **Grab These Bonds For 10% Yields** (SmartMoney)
- ➢ **Stocks That Pay You 5% Or More** (Kiplinger's Personal Finance)

It bothers me that these articles focus primarily on yields. Yes, stock dividends and bond yields are a significant component of market investment returns, but what the articles don't seem to mention is that where there is potential for returns, there is also potential for loss. For example, Money Magazine, which is loaded with advertisements from mutual fund companies, tells you that for safety you should use laddered certificates of deposit (CDs). Yeah right… have you checked the interest rates for CDs these days?

Just once, I would like to see a headline that reads, "Stocks That Pay You 5% or More or Could Lose 5% or More," followed by the subtitle, "Simple Gains – Compound Losses," but that wouldn't sell many magazines.

Jonathan Ping, who writes an online column titled "My Money Blog," agrees with my view of these attention-grabbing headlines. After he read a Kiplinger's article titled "Where to Find Top Yields," he had this to say: "I think these "yield fest" articles are written primarily to increase their own revenue, not the investment returns of their readers."

What is a seeker of sound and reasonable investment advice to do? For one, recognize that there are no absolutes when it comes to investing and wealth building, and there is almost always an alternative view. What fits one investor's needs may not fit another. What works for one portfolio may not be appropriate for another! It all depends on your individual needs, goals and values. Magazines that shout stock tips out at you from the rack are probably not the place to find strategies for a secure and safe retirement. One more thing: If you thumb through the magazine, you will see who is paying to have the articles published. You would have to be pretty naïve not to connect the dots between the advertisers and the editorial content of the magazine. Have you ever counted the number and types of adds in a magazine like Money? I counted 80-plus advertisements from mutual fund companies and the magazine articles all skewed toward mutual fund investing. Go figure.

## Investment Theatre on TV

Then there are the financial channels on TV. I confess I watch them from time to time. When you come in my office, you will see they are always on. While great entertainment, I don't recommend you watch them to learn how to invest. The program producers love to put two "analysts" side by side on a split screen and then let them duke it out verbally. The constant bickering and interrupting is enough to make you scramble for the "mute" button on the remote. It may be good television, but can you really take these people seriously?

There's one guy who comes on the screen wearing a funny hat, honking a bulb horn and blowing a slide whistle, for crying out loud. It would be funny if it weren't for the fact that he makes bold predictions and stock buying recommendations. One of the most egregious bad calls our boy with the funny hat and whistle ever made was shortly before the collapse of the large investment bank Bear Stearns in 2008. He screamed at the television audience in his hyperbolic style, "Bear Stearns is fine! Bear Stearns is fine!" The problem is that once in a while one of his picks will actually do well, which makes some people think he is able to predict the future. As I said, it would be easy for me to simply dismiss him as a "financial comedian" if it weren't for the fact that some folks I know of risked their hard-earned money on his advice and lost it.

## "Hot Stock Tips" (Scuttlebutt)

There's usually one in every office — the "coffee room stock tipper." The coffee room is where office workers gather for small talk and the "tipper" is the co-worker who wants to let you in on the ground floor of an investment that he or she has come across because a friend of someone who knows someone who knows someone else has whispered some secret information that no one else knows. The bottom line is, this stock is about to blow off the doors and you'd better get in quick before you miss the opportunity.

## Friends and Family Advice

I saw a cartoon recently where a little girl was behind a lemonade stand. The sign over her head said, "Lemonade — 25 cents, Investment Advice Free." It wouldn't surprise me to see that in real life because everybody these days seems to want to advise you on how to handle your money. Some of the most well-meaning folks, but some of the most misguided, are friends and relatives. When Chicago consulting firm Spectrum Group asked more than 400 people how they made investing decisions within their 401(k) retirement accounts, 44 percent of those under 35 and 21 percent overall said they turn to friends and relatives for advice. It reminds me of those friends-and-family mobile telephone deals. But do we really want our retirement security hinging on what Uncle Fred or Neighbor Bob have as their mutual fund choices? What's next? Polling your Facebook friends for advice?

Some people engage in what I call "taillight navigating." It's when you don't know where to go, so you just follow the taillights of whoever's in front of you. "Surely they know where they're going," you tell yourself. It sort of reminds you of those lemmings in the Walt Disney nature film "White Wilderness." The movie contains a scene depicting a mass lemming migration. Shockingly, it ends with thousands of these furry creatures running headlong off a cliff into the Arctic Ocean because they just followed the herd.

Some throw up their hands, paralyzed by too many conflicting opinions and opposing philosophies. They simply fail to plan. But that's not an acceptable option, either. My advice, dear reader, is that you take charge of your own financial future. Do your homework. Consult a professional. What do you do when you have a problem with your **health?** Ask your neighbor? Consult Uncle Fred, Neighbor Bob or Cousin Mary? Surf the TV channels or search the Internet? No, you consult a doctor. More than that, you consult a specialist who is fully trained and certified to answer questions and give you direction regarding whatever ails you. The same goes for concerns you have for your **wealth.** Read books on personal finance. Know how much you are spending, saving and earning. Know where you have your savings and **why** you have it there. Ask questions of your banker, or whoever represents the custodian in whose hands you have placed your "rainy day money." If you receive financial statements, open and read them; if you don't understand them, ask questions until you do. You wouldn't go to a doctor and say "Doc, it hurts, but you're the expert so I'm not telling where. You figure it out." We go to specialists from the time of pre-birth on to death. Pediatricians and geriatric doctors exist just as do general investors, brokers and income specialists.

## The World Is a Different Place

The investment world has changed in the last 20 years; don't let anyone tell you that it hasn't. If your broker or other financial professional is telling you that investing is the same today as in the 1980s and 1990s, he or she may be — how do I say this gracefully? — "unacquainted" with the facts.

They should rename the decade from 1990-2000, "The Roaring Nineties" from the standpoint of investing in the stock market. You literally could throw darts at the ticker symbols on the financial page, buy whatever the darts landed on and come out smelling like a rose. In fact, that actually happened. People once staged the publicity stunt using a trained chimpanzee to pick stocks. The 6-year-old female chimpanzee's name was Raven, and in 1999 she was given 10 darts to toss at a list of 133 Internet companies. This was during the days when any company ending with "dot-com" was considered to be on the cutting edge of technology and bound to produce profits eventually, even if there was no business plan and no visible pathway to earnings. The trained chimpanzee's stock picks produced a 213 percent gain. If she had actually been a fund manager, she would have been ranked as the 22$^{nd}$ best money manager in the country — better than more than 6,000 of her colleagues on Wall Street.

Many baby boomers retiring today remember those glory days of the 1990s as one of the longest economic expansions in the history of the American stock market. The euphoria produced during that time was so strong in the nostrils of the Wall Street bulls that they expected the happy days to never end. However, many continue to invest with a "buy-and-hold" strategy the same way they did in the 1980s and 1990s, and it just isn't working in today's financial times. What changed? Computer trading for one — as high-frequency trading has been a topic several times on the ever-popular television series "60 Minutes." The market has become volatile, just like a nervous woodland creature, jerking up and down to every whisper of a news event. Market reaction to world events is almost instantaneous. Computers have given institutional investors complex tools that were simply not around in the 1990s. All of this has given the market a different trading texture. At one time, "buy-and-hold" was virtually an investing creed and to preach otherwise was pure heresy. No more. Even the die-hard conservatives of the investment world are beginning to realize it. Permanently owning almost any asset has become too risky. Who would have thought that General Motors, which was considered at one time to be as solid as the U.S. dollar itself, would be standing before Congress with hat in hand asking for a handout in 2008? If your portfolio had included Hewlett Packard, Sears and

General Motors, who would have dreamed that trouble loomed on the horizon in 2000? But as Bob Dylan so prophetically sang in the early 1960s, "The times, they are a-changing."

It used to be, for example, that you could park your money in a mutual fund, set the autopilot and watch it grow. But in the "lost decade" of 2000-2010, the graphs tracking the movement of market indices were undulating like the tracks of a roller coaster. And just like on that thrill ride, the car always ends up back at square one — all that activity and no accomplishment, a flat line, no growth.

## Recovery Time from a Bear Market

The iconic symbol for a market on the upswing is the charging bull. The symbol that represents a market in correction mode is a giant bear, cautious and wary, plodding on all fours. Technically, a bear market has been defined as when the S&P index is down 20 percent or more over a two-month period. An investor with time on his or her side can weather the ups and downs of the stock market better than someone who is in or approaching retirement for ob-vious reasons. Here are some interesting statistics collected from Standard & Poor's:

- There have been 16 bear markets since 1929.
- A bear market comes along every 4.8 years.
- The average depth of decline in a bear market is 38.24 percent.
- On average, bear markets last 17 months.
- The average time it takes to break even (make up the losses) from a bear market is five years.

Think about that last one! Some recessions have been very brief, but they have also been very deep. Take the 1987 bear market, for example. It only lasted three months, but the S&P lost 33.5 percent. It took investors two years to re-cover from that two-month slide. Some may remember when the tech bubble burst, causing the bear market that lasted from March 2000 to October 2002. During that period, the S&P lost 49.1 percent, and it took investors a more than seven years to recover. No sooner had they recovered from that punch, however, than another knockout blow rocked the investment world.

I remember watching the numbers crawl across the bottom of the TV screen when on Sept. 29, 2008, the Dow Jones Industrial Average lost a whopping 777 points in one day. Officially, that bear market started in October 2007, and lasted throughout March 2009 — approximately 18 months — but it was the steepest decline since the Great Depression, and many are still recovering from it.

"But wait a minute," some might say. Hasn't the market bounced all the way back? As this book is written, that is a true statement. On Oct. 9, 2007, the Dow closed at its pre-recession all-time high of 14,164.43. On March 11, 2013, it closed at 14,254.38, taking five years to surpass its previous all-time record set in 2007. Since that time, the Dow surged to a record 18,024.17 on Dec. 23, 2014.

But what about individual investors? Consider the fact that few investors mirrored the exact movements of the market. Average Main Street Joe Investor hung in there too long out of hope and stubbornness, thinking that perhaps the storm would blow over and the ship would right itself. But when the pressure of losing everything got to him, he retreated to safety as an act of sheer preservation. Then, when the recovery finally did begin, he was so jaded that he missed a good portion of it — the once bitten, twice shy syndrome. The point is, when it comes to individually recovering from bear markets, you have to take into account the human element and figure into the picture the driving force behind any market — human emotions.

To illustrate recovery time from a market crash, it is helpful to look at the simple math. Let's say you have four quarters and take 50 percent of your quarters away. You now only have two quarters. I give you 50 percent of the remaining quarters back to you. How many quarters do you have? Three. To get back to having four quarters again, I have to give you back 100 percent of what I took away. Makes sense, doesn't it? And yet some have difficulty getting it straight when we talk about money in the stock market after a crash. In a very inflated and unrealistic example, let's say you have $100,000 in the market. The market goes down 50 percent and your holdings are reduced in value to

$50,000. If the market goes back up 50 percent, are you made whole again? Not by a long shot.

The market has to go up 100 percent before you completely recover what you lost.

# CHAPTER 3

# Average vs. Actual Returns

When people are touting an investment opportunity, they typically focus on the rate of return as the single most important thing to consider. The common notion is that the average rate of return is king and is to be considered as the standard by which we should judge any investment. It is true that a good rate of return, combined with compound interest, can work wonders when we are building our retirement nest egg. But it is one of the least understood facets of investing.

There's an axiom that says, "If all you have is a hammer, everything begins to look like a nail." Advisors who have a limited tool box and only deal in securities for retirement planning like to point to the average rate of return of what they are selling, whether it be a mutual fund or a portfolio grouping. The idea they put forth is that over time, if the average rate of return is, say, 8 percent, then it is worth taking a risk because when the smoke clears and the highs and lows are flattened out, the gains will outweigh the losses. Sounds good, but in order for this to work, they have to go back a number of years to make sure they catch the 1980s and 1990s when the numbers help the average considerably. The only problem is that average rates of return have little to do with accumulating money.

What is the formula for calculating average rate of return? Simply add up the return for each year, both positive and negative, and then divide by the number of years. Let's say you had $1,000 and that increased by 100 percent. You would have $2,000. Simple. Now let's say that in the following year that $2,000 decreased by 60 percent. How much do you have? That's right, $800. So your ***average rate of return*** for the period is 20 percent. But did you actually get a 20 percent return on your money? Hardly! Your $1,000 is down to $800! It's not the return **on** your money that is nearly important as the return **of** your money. You can't spend average rates of return. You can only spend money. While your average rate of return may have been 20 percent, the actual rate of return was negative 10 percent. When you are talking about ROI (return on investments), you cannot use averages due to the fact that when you get a negative number, it skews the picture.

**Here's an example:**

Let's say someone had a portfolio worth $100,000 and in the first year it increased by 10 percent. The second year, it decreased by 10 percent. The portfolio seesawed back and forth like this for 10 years, gaining 10 percent then losing 10 percent. You end up with five years of 10 percent gains and five years of 10 percent declines. How much would you have in your account?

Some will answer $100,000, because you had as many gains as you had losses, so it leveled out. You're back where you started, aren't you? No. Let's do the math.

50 (total percent gained) minus 50 (percent lost) = zero
Divided by 10 years, that is a ZERO percent rate of return.

But when you do the "actual" instead of the "average" rate of return, you must take the $100,000, add 10 percent to it, and you now have $110,000. See what I mean? Now all the calculations you do after this must take into account the changed amount. If you take away 10 percent from this changed amount ($110,000), you are taking away a larger portion than from the original number ($100,000). You are actually taking away $11,000. Now your account is down to $99,000. See how important the timing of returns is?

**When** those increases or decreases occurred plays a big part to play in how those numbers affected the value of the account. In the above illustration, using $100,000 with five increases of 10 percent and five decreases of 10 percent over a 10-year span, you ended up with $95,099 in your account. The difference is ***losses.***

## Sequence of Returns Critical in Retirement

The second issue is how the distribution phase impacts the account value for someone who has to live off that retirement account. Timing is extremely critical. As we have already pointed out, we are more vulnerable to market risk as we get older because we have less time to recover. The risk is heightened even more for those who must withdraw money from an account that is still parked in the market. The order in which the returns occur is critical. While the account is accumulating, the order of returns doesn't matter as much, but as soon as you begin withdrawals, everything changes. If you retire to negative years first, like many did in 2001-2002 or 2008-2009 for example, you will run out of money much sooner than if you get positive returns first and have negative returns later. The reason is quite simple: The losses in the negative years are compounded by the withdrawals, requiring a much greater return to recover what you lost. At my firm, Retirement Solutions Group, Inc., we look at ROI not as "return on investment" but rather "reliability of income." In retirement, it is the return of your money that should be your No. 1 focus in a consistent and inflation-adjusted fashion.

The following example shows a hypothetical sequence of returns of two investors, Brother 1 and Brother 2. They both invested the same amount of money, $500,000, and they both had identical "average" rates of return at 8 percent. They each withdrew exactly the same amount each year, $25,000, plus 3 percent incrementally for inflation. But look what a difference the sequence of the returns, specifically the losses, makes.

| START BROTHER 1: | 1998 |
|---|---|
| START BROTHER 2: | 2000 |
| PREMIUM: | $600,000.00 |
| ANNUAL WD: | $40,000.00 |

| YEAR | S&P RETURN | BROTHER 1 | BROTHER 2 |
|---|---|---|---|
| 1990 | 27.25% | | |
| 1991 | -6.56% | | |
| 1992 | 26.31% | | |
| 1993 | 4.46% | | |
| 1994 | 7.06% | | |
| 1995 | -1.54% | | |
| 1996 | 34.11% | | |
| 1997 | 20.26% | | |
| 1998 | 31.01% | $733,656.00 | |
| 1999 | 26.67% | $878,654.06 | |
| 2000 | 19.53% | $1,002,443.19 | $669,368.00 |
| 2001 | -10.14% | $864,851.45 | $565,550.08 |
| 2002 | -13.04% | $717,290.82 | $457,018.35 |
| 2003 | -23.37% | $519,007.96 | $319,561.16 |
| 2004 | 26.38% | $605,370.26 | $353,309.40 |
| 2005 | 8.99% | $616,197.04 | $341,475.91 |
| 2006 | 3.00% | $593,482.95 | $310,520.19 |
| 2007 | 13.62% | $628,867.33 | $307,365.04 |
| 2008 | 3.53% | $609,654.35 | $276,803.03 |
| 2009 | -38.49% | $350,394.39 | $145,657.54 |
| 2010 | 23.45% | $383,181.88 | $130,434.24 |
| 2011 | 12.78% | $387,040.52 | $101,991.73 |
| 2012 | 0.00% | $347,040.52 | $61,991.73 |
| 2013 | 13.41% | $348,214.65 | $24,940.82 |
| 2014 | 29.60% | $399,446.19 | -$19,516.69 |

The point of all this is, regardless of how accurate you may be in projecting an average return, there is not a direct correlation between that number and how much actual income will end up in your pocket, or how long your income will last you in retirement. It all has to do with the sequence of returns.

# CHAPTER 4

# Plan With Purpose

When you stop and think about what money really is, it will make your head hurt. The cash in your pocket is only paper with numbers on it or a metal disk with artwork in relief stamped upon it. We can only carry so much of that stuff on our person. Where is the rest of our wealth? More numbers on paper in the form of the bottom line on a statement or digits on a computer screen. Even real estate has to be backed up by a paper of some sort and kept as an entry on a courthouse ledger.

The value we attach to money is ethereal too. Just ask those who have lived through the hyperinflation of the late 1970s and early 1980s. Not that he was to blame, but Jimmy Carter was president when the value of a dollar became 75 cents almost overnight. So the real question, when it comes to money, is what do you want it to do for you? That's what I choose to work with when it comes to helping clients forge their financial future — not just a return percentage, although that is important, but having your money accomplish your financial and life goals.

If I could build this in cinder-block letters the size of the Hollywood sign and paint them neon orange, I would: ***Without the purpose you attach to it, wealth is merely numbers on paper.***

## Financial Readiness Sadly Lacking

I saw a T-shirt the other day with the slogan: "Thinking is hard work... which explains why so few people do it." Planning successfully for one's retirement first requires significant thought. It may sound like I am stating the obvious here, but research shows that many do not give their financial future the thought it requires.

I recently saw a cartoon depicting a little old lady unwrapping a candy bar. It was obvious that she had been saving the treat for just the right time, and now, her moment had come. The caption read, "I'm going to retire and live off my savings. What I'll do on the *second day*, I have no idea." I had to chuckle and shake my head. A one-day retirement plan! But if research is to be believed, that's not too far off the mark for many of those approaching retirement. Like a motorist in a thick fog, their retirement visibility does not reach very far in front of them.

Do you know how much income you will need in retirement? Have you estimated how much it is going to cost to house, feed and clothe you and your spouse while allowing you to remain in your comfortable home? Do you know how much it will take to see you through the next 20 or even 30 years of unemployment? Do you know where that money will come from and whether you can depend on it being available to you when you need it? Have you planned for the rising health care costs and the possibility that, at some point, you may need long-term care? Do you want to leave a legacy to your heirs or to your favorite charity? If so, do you know how you intend to do it?

In my informal surveys, I have come to the conclusion that many know how they are going to make it through the first 10 years, but they are scared sleepless when they think about living 20 or 30 years on the nest egg they have managed to accumulate. Like the little old lady in the cartoon, the vast majority of people seem to choose the "Oh well, it will all work out somehow" strategy.

This was confirmed recently when I was doing a little research for one of my Saturday morning radio talk shows and came across these startling statistics:

- 35% of American workers have no plan for retirement whatsoever.
- 36% of Americans do not save anything for retirement.
- 35% of Americans over age 65 will rely solely on Social Security in retirement.
- Nearly 60% of Americans say they plan to retire by age 65, but nearly the same percentage fear they will never save enough to do it.
- The average savings of 50-year-old males are only $43,797.

- The average length of retirement is 18 years.
- The total cost of a couple over 65 to pay for medical treatment over a 20-year span is $215,000.
- 13% of Americans are 65 or older.
- 6,000 Americans turn 65 every day.
- If you need $4,000 per month in income when you retire, you need to have $666,783 in savings for 20 years of retirement and $848,601 in savings for 30 years of retirement.

(Sources: U.S. Census Bureau, Saperston Companies, Bankrate, Jan. 1, 2014)

I had already deduced that most people approaching retirement are winging it, but this study made it crystal clear. American author and motivational speaker Zig Ziglar was right when he said "Many people spend more time planning a two-week vacation than they do planning their life. One of the most important things you can do to shape your future is to have clearly defined written goals and a plan to achieve them. After that, it is simply a matter of working on that plan each day."

## Retirement Readiness

A retirement readiness survey taken by the Transamerica Center for Retirement Studies released in 2016 included a sampling from all three age segments of what it called our "three-generation workforce." Popular culture has given each age group a clever name — baby boomers, Generation Xers and millennials.

- Baby boomer: born 1946-1964
- Generation X: born 1965-1978
- Millennial: born 1979-1996

Would it really surprise you to learn that millennials give little thought to their retirement? It did not shock me. The tail end of this group is only 19 years old as I write this. What were you thinking about when you were 19? I was just getting my feet wet in the Navy. Retirement was for old people.

Boomers and Gen-Xers should know better, however. At this writing, Generation X is approaching 50 and baby boomers are already past the half-century mark. All three groups were lumped together in the survey and less than one out of 10 had used a retirement calculator to estimate their retirement savings needs. If I may be so bold, the last two groups, especially those 50 and older, need to pull your heads out from under the sheets to see what's making those scary shadows on the wall. Time is rapidly slipping away!

# The Secret

Transamerica's retirement readiness study made this profound observation:

> "One of the most important secrets to attaining retirement readiness is having a well-defined written strategy about retirement income needs, costs and expenses, and risk factors."

The survey revealed that most folks were simply guessing.

It reminds me of a commercial I saw a couple of years ago. I can't remember the sponsor, but the 30-second spot had to do with "finding your number" — the amount of money you would need to have saved before you could safely retire. The setting was a tree-lined sidewalk in a typical American neighborhood. We see a man walking his dog and — as bizarre as it sounds — he is carrying under his right arm a big orange number. The camera angle does not let you see exactly what the number is, but it appears to be a little over a million. As unwieldy as the large cardboard number is, people pass by and wave as if it is perfectly normal behavior for someone to be walking around carrying a big orange number. That's the hook to the commercial, of course. You want to see why he has the number and what it means.

In the next scene, we learn that the dog-walking, number carrier's name is Clark. "Hey Clark," says a man who is obviously Clark's neighbor. "What'cha got there?" he says, pointing to the big orange number. Sitting on top of the hedge the neighbor is trimming is a big purple word, "Gazillion."

"It's my number," says Clark. "It's the amount I need to save to retire the way I want."

Ah! Now we know what the number is all about! The camera swings back to the hedge trimmer and his nonsensical number, "Gazillion."

"Is that your number ... Gazillion?" The dog walker asks the hedge trimmer.

"Yeah, gazillion, bazillion … it's just a guesstimation," shrugs the neighbor.

The dog-walking neighbor scratches his head and frowns. "How do you plan for **that**?"

The hedge-trimmer guy laughs nervously and says, "I just blindly throw money at it and hope something good happens."

"So, you really don't have a plan at all," Clark says, reproachfully.

"I really don't," confesses the chastened neighbor as he continues snipping his hedge.

I am not usually a big fan of TV commercials, but this one deserves an Emmy for so effectively making the point that guessing at your retirement number is foolish and the smart thing to do is ferret out the facts and come up with your real number.

## Finding Your Number

What about you? What's your number? How much must you have accumulated in order to sleep well at night knowing that you have enough to pay your bills and maintain your independence for 20, maybe 30 years or more?

As a retirement income planner, I usually back into that number. Determine your budget first. Project your expenses, and figure in all the contingencies. Identify your income sources. Nail an expected retirement date, and see if you have enough to press the big red "I Quit" button at work and enter the retirement zone. If you come up short, it means you have to go back to the drawing board. Any number of actions may be required to get you to your number. Save more, spend less, earn more and work longer.

The great thing about planning is that it lays out for you the road ahead. The fog lifts and your visibility is to infinity, not just to the end of your headlights. In the commercial, Clark the dog-walker was obviously the smart one because he took the time to think things out while his hedge-trimming neighbor just had a lazy, hazy guess as to how much he needed to have tucked away. There is an axiom: "If you fail to plan, you plan to fail." No one actually plans to fail, of course. That's just what happens by default.

In the Transamerica survey, nearly 90 percent of workers said they were, like the hedge trimmer, just guessing at their retirement "number." Boomers and millennials guessed on average $800,000 and Gen-Xers guessed $1 million. But there was no connection to the facts.

---

# Retirement or Transition?

One challenge clouding the issue of planning is the word "retire" itself. As mentioned in the preface, according to the Merriam-Webster dictionary, the word "retire" means "to withdraw." But completely withdrawing from secular work is no longer the picture that plays in the minds of workers when they think of retirement. Many baby boomers and Generation Xers plan to work past age 65 or do not plan to retire at all. And it's not always because they need the income.

As a class, modern seniors pride themselves on being active and fit. What is it they say? Sixty is the new 40? Many of them may be like me. I love what I'm doing. I love helping people plan their financial futures. I love keeping up with all the latest research. It keeps me invigorated and makes me feel young and alive! I am not saying I will not spend more time golfing or traveling as I cross the finish line of each future decade, but I hope to always spend a little time in the office keeping connected with my community.

I get the sense that we are actually experiencing a new trend in retirement, and it does not surprise me that the baby boomer generation is behind it. After all, boomers rocked the world with music that was "cutting edge" for its time — Elvis Presley, the Beatles and The Rolling Stones. Boomers were the ones who forever altered the social landscape with civil rights and women's rights. They left their mark in economics by demanding competitive money market funds, multi-purpose insurance products and global investing. For them, the idea of just fading away, which is what the word retirement connotes, just does not work. Perhaps the lexicographers will come up with a new word to replace "retirement." How about using the word "*transition*" instead? This word might better describe what is actually happening in this stage of life — transitioning from working years to years of leisure.

"So Bob, when do you plan to *transition*?"

"I will *transition* in four more months."

"Are they going to throw you a *transition* party?"

"I sure hope so. You only *transition* once!"

"What do you plan to do when you *transition?*"

'I will probably still work at the parts of my job that I like... you know, helping the new kids climbing the ladder... show them the ropes."

"What about after that?"

"Well, at some point in my *transition,* I plan to scale back to maybe 20 hours a week."

I like this idea of replacing the word "retirement" with the word "transition," but it may be hard to convince the dictionary people — although they do let in a few new words each year (Google is now an official verb). But it may be hard to get the definition completely changed. However, modern retirement is all about transition, isn't it? "Changing from one state or condition to another," as the dictionary defines it.

Boomers and Gen-Xers seem to want a more gradual change, going from full-time work to leisure time, not a sudden stop. This kind of transition reminds me of my Navy days. When a big ship had to navigate from one body of water to another and the two bodies of water were at different levels, the ship went through locks. The vessel entered a fixed chamber and watertight doors closed behind it. Operators of the locks slowly pumped water into the chamber (or drained water out) until the ship became level with the body of water it needed to enter. In some places like the Panama Canal, it required a series of locks and connecting canals to be accomplished. Similarly, more and more modern retirees are working long after their 65th birthdays. Some start second careers, this time doing something they always wanted to do, such as turning an interest or hobby into gainful employment. Others work part time. Some volunteer because they want to remain active and productive in their communities. Transitional employment is becoming a bigger piece of the retirement puzzle, and I predict the trend will continue.

## Transition Employment

If the idea of working past retirement age appeals to you, the Transamerica study lists six things you might want to consider to help position yourself for transitional work opportunities when they come along.

- Take steps to stay healthy.
- Focus on performing well where you are now.
- Network and meet people who are doing what you WANT to do.
- Actively search NOW for the opportunities you want later.
- Go back to school to learn NEW skills.
- Keep your current job skills up to date.

# Planning for Contingencies

If you are normal, you probably went through a phase as a child of being afraid of the dark. Any unexplained noise — a creaking floorboard, a tree limb tapping on a windowpane or any random bump in the night could fill you with terror. What we feared, of course, was not the absence of light but the unknown. We were uncomfortable because we could not see what was there. Psychologists tell us that this is a healthy emotion and that we should be wary of unseen hazards. They say this type of fear is a carryover from the nights our ancestors spent with animals on the prowl beyond the glow of their campfire.

In retirement planning, illuminating contingencies — things we cannot see but might happen — is also a necessity. We make allowances for them, perhaps not perfectly, but as best we can. It is just smart to provide protection from such things as failing health and inflation, for example, if at all possible.

# Inflation

Increased longevity puts retirees at greater risk for inflation. Inflation works like compound interest. Compound interest is a beautiful thing when it is working for us, but once we retire and it takes the form of inflation, it can be one of our worst enemies. Let me illustrate with the Rule of 72. Divide 72 by the inflation rate and you will see how long it will take for prices to double. So, for instance, if inflation holds at 3 percent and you currently need $45,000 a year to live on, in 24 years (72÷3=24) you will need $90,000 to maintain your standard of living. If inflation averages 4 percent, in just 18 years (72÷ 4=18) you will need $90,000. If inflation averages 5 percent, in 14.4 years ($72 \div 5 = 14.4$) you will need $90,000.

As of the writing of this book, U.S. inflation is holding steady at a manageable 2 percent. It has been at an all-time low for the past five years. But in the 25-year span from 1967 to 1992, inflation consistently held at around 3 percent in all but one year, 1980, when the inflation rate peaked at 14.8 percent and interest rates peaked at 18 percent. We hope that doesn't happen again. But do you really believe that we will be able to maintain such a tame rate of inflation as we currently enjoy for the next 30 years? I doubt it.

Retirees typically spend their money on inflation-sensitive products and services. There is no way around this. Everyone needs food, clothing and shelter. The bottom line is no matter how much income you begin retirement with, you will need more as time goes by. How much more, we do not know. Prudent retirement planning dictates that we plan on at least a 2.5 percent to 3 percent rate of inflation just in case. It's just one more piece of the retirement planning puzzle.

## How Much of Your Retirement Do You Want Guaranteed?

Today more than ever, retirees are becoming more responsible for creating their own retirement paychecks to supplement Social Security benefits and pensions. Corporate pension programs have been on the decline for the past four decades, and Social Security is seeing more pressure every day to provide benefits. On top of that, one major concern for most Americans is outliving and outspending their savings. Retirees today want to create paychecks that will last as long as they do. To create a lifetime series of income payments, or "paychecks," retirees have to sit down and have a strategy on how to create those "paychecks."

There are a few schools of thought on how you provide someone with a lifetime income. Many advisors rely on the "old school" methods of utilizing diversified portfolios of mutual funds and dividend-paying equity funds, bond laddering or even laddering CDs. By following those methods, you may have a good shot at receiving an income you can't outlive. However, you run the risk that there are no guarantees in these types of investments. A catastrophic event like 9/11, or a recession like 2008, would dramatically affect the yield, or income, you would be able to take from your portfolio. A typical response to a market "correction" is to adjust your withdrawals based on market conditions and portfolio value. In plain English, you would have to take a pay cut.

The "new school" method involves using the correct tool for each job. By opening the toolboxes of both the investment world and insurance world, you can create a guaranteed lifetime income that can help address inflation and allows the funds remaining in your investment portfolio to continue to be used to possibly grow your wealth. The insurance industry has created annuity products that protect your principal while creating a personal income stream in efficient ways today. The remaining available assets can be kept in the market and play to the strength of having money exposed to appropriate risk and allocation strategies.

In our modern economy, knowing where to go for income and where to go for growth is simpler once you decide how much of your income you want guaranteed and how much you want exposed to risk.

# Health Care

Unexpected medical expense is another contingency. We can't foresee our need, or the lack thereof, for long-term care or assisted living. But, we can acknowledge the statistics and plan for it to the best of our ability. The statistic used most often in everything I read says that more than 70 percent of Americans over the age of 65 will need long-term care services at some point in their lives. So says the U.S. Department of Health and Human Services, anyway. Another HHS statistic is that anyone reaching the age of 65 years has a 40 percent chance of entering a nursing home, with a 20 percent chance of staying there for at least five years.

If you are thinking that Medicare will absorb the related costs, you're wrong. Medicare only covers up to 100 days of long-term care, but only if you have previously been in a hospital for three consecutive days prior to needing long-term services. Additionally, only the first 20 days are covered in full; the remaining 80 days require a daily co-payment. Medicaid does cover it, but you have to be a pauper and a ward of the state to qualify. If you require extended long-term care in a nursing home, you may end up a pauper. The HHS pegs the average national cost of a semi-private room in a nursing home at $72,270 a year, or $198 a day. A private room is $219 a day, or $79,935 a year. These are average costs, bear in mind. In large cities like New York and Boston, it is not uncommon for the expense to exceed $100,000 annually.

---

# Long-Term Care

One reason people overlook long-term care is because they misunderstand Medicare and Medicaid. Once they take a peek into the guidelines, they are shocked to find that Medicare does NOT pay for long-term care. It only pays for acute care. Medicaid will pay for long-term care but only after you "spend down" your assets. Another option is to purchase long-term care insurance. Buying it sooner rather than later won't necessarily save you any money on the policy, but it might be easier on your budget. If this seems confusing, just stick with me.

The book "10 Things to Know About Planning Your Retirement Income" had this to say: "A policy that pays out $100 a day for three years would cost an average 55-year-old $709 in annual premiums. That same policy would cost a typical 65-year-old $1,342." The cost practically doubles by waiting. Because you hadn't paid premiums in the earlier years, the premium for the policy is proportionately the same; however, you were not covered and if your health changes there is the possibility that you will not be able to get a policy when you want. So the policy that I took out when I was 30 will cost me about the same as an 80-year-old who pays for a policy for, say, only five years before using it. The difference is they will pay the premium in a little over five years and I will have more than 50 years to pay down the same premium.

There are many choices in long-term health care, and it pays to bone up on the details, especially because even the above details are averages and not hard quotes for every situation, and you'll want information that is more specific to your particular needs. AARP makes this easy by providing a long-term care calculator on its website. Just to illustrate, at the time this book is being written, I keyed Lawrence, Kansas, into the search box to compare costs locally.

| TYPE OF CARE | LAWRENCE, KANSAS |
|---|---|
| Nursing Home *(Private Room)* 2 years | 2014 cost: $ 70,445 |
| | 2015 cost: $ 73,967 |
| | **Total cost for all years: $ 144,412** |
| Nursing Home *(Semi-Private)* 2 years | 2014 cost: $ 62,233 |
| | 2015 cost: $ 65,345 |
| | **Total cost for all years: $ 127,578** |
| Assisted Living *(Private Room)* 2 years | 2014 cost: $ 56,040 |
| | 2015 cost: $ 58,842 |
| Adult Day Care *7 day(s)/week* | 2014 cost: $27,300 (in Wichita) |
| Home Health Aid *7 hr(s)/week* | 2014 cost: $ 6,643 |
| | 2015 cost: $ 6,975 |
| Homemaker Services *7 hr(s)/week* | 2014 cost: $ 6,188 |
| | 2015 cost: $ 6,497 |

As you can see, there is a huge difference between the costs and types of services. The more you know about this, the greater your chances of structuring your retirement plan so that it matches your goals and desires. My motto is, "As much as possible, have it YOUR way." Of course, that takes planning with a purpose! It's our opinion that everyone needs to assess his or her potential long-term care needs. We can help you analyze different options that can best assist you in dealing with the related future costs. There are four ways to plan for long-term care costs:

1. **Traditional Long-Term Care (LTC) Insurance:** Must be able to health qualify at the time of purchase. Plans that comply with state guidelines may help protect assets if the need for state assistance ever arises. Options such as amount of coverage, length of coverage and inflation protection can be reviewed to find the right fit for your overall planning needs.

2. **Asset Based:** Utilizing monies currently held in personal savings to cover cost of LTC. If you have a strategy to supplement your monthly income if needed, then this may be a workable plan.

3. **Life Insurance Based:** Utilizing income value to cover the cost of long-term care.

4. **Life Insurance With LTC Benefits:** Life insurance policies that offer a benefit if long-term care needs arise, and a death benefit if the LTC portion of the policy is not utilized.

# A Written Plan

You heard the one about the difference between the pig and the chicken and a bacon-and-egg breakfast, didn't you? The chicken was involved, but the pig was committed! Few of us would believe that a couple was seriously committed to the project of building a house if they never got around to drawing up the blueprints. Once the plans are put on paper, however, we can sense a new level of commitment. Suddenly, anyone can see the layout, the support structures and the design. Putting it on paper adds substance and dimension to the project. Then, the couple can ask, "How much is this thing going to cost?" Lastly, they can begin to bring their reality (limited by their budget, space and time) in line with their vision. Even if they have to make some adjustments, in the end they can build a home they can live with and love.

In my experience as a professional retirement income planner, until people clearly define what they really need and put a plan in writing, retirement is merely a far off dream or dreaded nightmare. But once a plan is written, people commit and get empowered as they see their vision becoming a reality. Is it hard work? Of course! But together we prove that it is achievable.

# Replacement Income

Retirement is different for everyone, as you may choose to play golf every day, spend time with the grandkids or start another job for profit or charity. Whatever your choices, remember every day is Saturday, and that's the day of the week we typically spend the most money. It's been said historically that you don't have to replace 100 percent of your wages once you retire to maintain your standard of living. Traditionally, 65 percent of your pre-retirement wages will suffice because the costs associated with working, such as transportation and work-related clothing, are no longer part of your budget. However, increased longevity really throws a monkey wrench into the historical plan for several reasons.

Obviously, it takes a larger chunk of change to fund a 20- or 30-year retirement than the average 13-year retirement of yesteryear. For better or worse, with better nutrition and health care, there is a real possibility that you could live to be 90 or 100.

Unfortunately, lately we have not been experiencing the best of times financially. For those on the cusp of retirement, the Great Recession (statistically pinpointed to have lasted from December 2007 through March 2009) really took its toll. While economists believe that it is now behind us, not everyone is buying that line of thinking. In the 2016 Transamerica poll, while most baby boomers, Generation Xers and millennials felt that they were recovering financially, only 20 percent felt they had fully recovered and 25 percent of the baby boomers felt they may never recover. All three generations felt they would have a harder time, financially, in retirement than their respective parents.

As my father, Robert Becker, often said to me when I was growing up, "It is what it is." In other words, it is better to face the facts and deal with reality than to ignore it. So what are the experts recommending? First, do not take chances with your replacement income money. The purpose of replacement income is to see you through all of your retirement years. The Ernst & Young study subtitled "The Likelihood of Outliving Their Assets" suggested this, "Focus on increasing retirement savings and vehicles that provide **a guaranteed lifetime income stream**." This product does exist and we will talk more about it in a subsequent chapter, so stay tuned.

The other bit of advice that is sometimes a bitter taste of reality is, "We just can't get there from here." Sometimes the truth is like medicine. It may be hard to swallow at times, but it's better than ignorance or, worse yet, lies. You may have to either reduce your standard of living now and plow the difference into retirement savings each year or expect to outlive your assets. In the rare case that a married couple is covered by an employer-based defined benefit pension,

# CHAPTER 5

# LTC, Medicare and Asset Protection

I t's time to battle the long-term care monster. Just the thought of long-term care frightens people. The media doesn't help. They sometimes feed that fright by carelessly tossing out numbers without tying them to facts. Yes, long-term care is expensive, but did you know that 92 percent of people who need LTC need it for less than three years? We can handle that and make a plan for addressing it. What if you happen to draw the short straw and end up being the rare case needing 20 years of long-term care? You will likely deplete your cash reserves and Medicaid will take over, which is why you pay taxes. In any event, you won't be kicked to the curb. Even in that worst-case scenario, there are some simple things you can do to pass on a modest legacy if that is important to you.

What I'm saying is to please resist the urge to view LTC like it's the Lon Chaney in a werewolf suit from his classic "Wolfman" movies — you know he's out there (eerie music), but who's going to be next? True enough, LTC is an asset-eating monster, but we can get the upper hand by planning it to death.

Long-term care is a broad-brush term we use to describe custodial and/or skilled care provided for more than 90 days. Treatment is given to individuals whose condition likely will not improve. It covers the gamut from bedridden patients in skilled nursing facilities (nursing homes) to occasional visits by a home health care nurse to someone recovering from a fractured limb. I find that most people have a story to tell about LTC. Someone in his or her family either is receiving or has received some type of long-term care or short-term care.

My maternal grandmother started showing signs of Alzheimer's before I went into the Navy. By the time I was discharged, she had lost her ability to speak. This was extremely devastating for me. As a kid, I loved to listen to her tell stories. Alzheimer's stole a little piece of my grandmother every day, and there is no cure for the disease. While it saddens me that I will never hear that kind, sweet voice again, I am comforted by the knowledge that she was well cared for in a long-term care facility.

My paternal grandmother is 98 years old and is living near us in an assisted living community. As this is written, she is nearly a centenarian and can, with a little help, still take care of herself! Amazing! We moved her from Florida to Kansas so she would be closer to us. I have to laugh about the fact that she has been near us for eight years now but still thinks she is visiting! I spent the better part of 10 years as a caregiver, while trying to raise our son Dylan; I had to take care of all household duties while building my planning firm. This eventually led to a breaking point where I had to choose, for my son and myself, another path.

Several years ago, an acquaintance learned his father had fallen and broken his hip. Surgery to repair the fracture was successful, and his dad was moved into a skilled care facility. Sadly, before three months had lapsed, he passed away. I share this to illustrate that his stay in the nursing home lasted less than three months. That's as long as the stay of 68 percent of people entering a nursing home. According to one AARP study, only 17 percent stay more than a year, and only 7 percent stay more than three years. I'm not saying we shouldn't prepare ourselves for this possibility, quite the opposite, but peel your fingers off the armrest, uncoil and relax. The fact is you now have more options than ever before and there's even a strategy for naysayers who absolutely refuse to pay for insurance they may never need.

## Long-Term Care (LTC) — When You Need It

Nursing home care or facility-based care becomes a concern when you go to the hospital with a serious illness or injury and the doctor will not release you

to go home. According to the National Association of Health Data Organization, here are the top 10 reasons people need LTC.

1. Fractured bones
2. Recovering from an illness, injury or surgery
3. Rehabilitation
4. Alzheimer's disease and dementia
5. Multiple sclerosis (MS)
6. Parkinson's disease
7. Heart disease
8. Strokes
9. Head injuries
10. Obesity and chronic or terminal medical conditions

If you have Medicare, as do most people over 65, and you are thinking that
it covers confinement in a nursing home, think again. Medicare is great, but it
will only pay for the first 20 days of LTC fully and days 21 through 100 with a
co-pay that changes annually. The co-pays are available on Medicare.gov. There
are three restrictions that have to be met in order for Medicare to pay:

- You have had a recent prior **hospital** stay of at least **three days**.
- You are admitted to a **certified nursing facility within 30 days** of
  your prior hospital stay.
- You need **skilled care** such as skilled nursing services, physical therapy, or other types of therapy.
  (www.LongTermCare.gov/medicare)

The first 20 days of care in this situation is referred to as "**skilled care**," and
you can receive it in many different settings, including a nursing home or rehabilitation center. So, to reiterate, Medicare will pay 100 percent of your costs
for the first 20 days. The idea is that if your condition does not improve in 90
days, you will need custodial care, and that is not in Medicare's wheelhouse.
Here is the key paragraph from the official literature on Medicare and Medicaid
provided by the U.S. Department of Health and Human Services:

> *"Medicare doesn't cover custodial care if it is the only kind of care you need. Custodial care is care that helps you with usual daily activities like getting in and out of bed, eating, bathing, dressing and using the bathroom. It may also include care that most people do themselves, like using eye drops, oxygen, and taking care of colostomy or bladder catheters. Custodial care is often given in a nursing facility... Generally, skilled care is available only for a short time after a hospitalization. Custodial care may be needed for a much longer period of time."*

As I write this in October 2015, Medicare will pay **some** of your costs for days 21 through 100. You pay up to $152 per day, and Medicare will pay the rest. The term for this is "**intermediate care**," and you can receive it at the same facility. After the 100th day, it is categorized as "**custodial care**," and you are responsible for 100 percent of the costs.

Medicare also pays for the services listed below for a **limited time** when your doctor says they are medically necessary to treat an illness or injury:

- Skilled nursing care that is part-time or intermittent.
- Services provided by a Medicare-certified home health agency, such as physical therapy, occupational therapy and speech-language pathology that your doctor orders for a limited number of days only.
- Medical social services to help cope with issues that result from an illness.
- Medical supplies and durable medical equipment like wheelchairs and walkers. You pay 20 percent of the Medicare-approved amount for durable equipment.

Even though this benefit is designed to be short-term, as long as these services remain medically necessary and your doctor reorders them every 60 days, there is no limit on how long you can receive them. Medicare also covers Medicare-approved hospice care if you are not expected to live more than six months. This includes medications for pain relief, symptom-control and support services. You have some options here. You can receive hospice care in your home, in a hospice care facility or in a nursing home if you already live there.

In May 2015, I watched the strongest person I've ever known, my mother Fran, go out on her own terms. She chose to go to the Kansas Hospice House like her best friend, my Aunt Marlene, did four years prior. I cannot say enough good things about their services in our time of need.

While it is comforting to know all the things that Medicare will pay for, don't overlook what it doesn't pay for as well. **Medicare doesn't pay for ANY LTC after the 100th day.** If I am repeating myself, it is because I have found that most people who come into my office for retirement planning are under the impression that Medicare will cover LTC. Perhaps it is because Medicare and Medicaid both start with the same prefix. Medicaid does step in and cover nursing home care after your resources are completely drained away and you are a pauper.

When someone needs help performing the normal activities of daily living — known in the medical and insurance community as ADLs — these are not considered medical needs. The six ADLs typically are specified as bathing, continence, dressing, eating, toileting and transferring. Since they are not "medical" needs, it is only logical that medical insurance (which is what Medicare is) would not pay for these things.

However, most privately issued long-term care insurance policies DO cover all three levels of care: skilled care, intermediate care and custodial care. They also can give you more control over where you will receive the care, such as at home or in an assisted living community. Even if you need nursing home care, you can choose the home of your choice because you are not limited to the Medicare-approved list. You should check your specific policy for details.

So what are the odds that you'll actually need LTC? Well, according to the National Clearinghouse for Long-Term Care Information, after turning age 65, we each have a 70 percent chance of needing LTC in our lifetime. The older you become, the greater the percentage. As I mentioned earlier, traditional LTC insurance is not the only option out there. But because it is a popular option, we are going to take a look at it first.

# Traditional Long-Term Care (LTC) Insurance

No one likes to be told what to do. We value our freedom of choice. That is one of the main benefits of LTC insurance. You decide who will take care of you and how. Another added benefit is not putting the burden on your family and friends. For most policies, when you can no longer do two of the six ADLs mentioned above, policy benefits are triggered. Depending on the policy or coverage you choose, you may be allowed to receive care in your home, a nursing home, an assisted living community, hospice or even an adult daycare facility. This care is evolving all the time. I would not be surprised if even more options became available in the next few years.

One level of care is skilled care. If you have an illness or disability, medical professionals such as registered nurses or therapists will assist you with hands-on or standby care. People with cognitive disorders also need protection, supervision and verbal reminders. According to an AARP study, this population accounts for nearly half of the nursing home residents. Of course, care has to be ordered by a physician, and a plan has to be put in place to receive insurance payments.

Personal care, or custodial care, helps you do the ADLs, and it is much less involved and, therefore, less expensive than skilled care.

If you flip back to the last chapter, to the six types of LTC and the costs, you'll see what I mean. In my neck of the woods, a private nursing home costs over 10 times as much as a home health aide. This is likely true no matter where you live. I could write an entire book on LTC insurance alone. What I will do, however, is give you a few pointers as you consider a purchase. Then we will answer the big question: How much does it cost?

# Compare Policies Before You Purchase

Not all LTC policies are created equal. Some policies have considerably higher premiums for essentially the same coverage. Long-term care has been a killer for insurance companies. The actuaries thought there would be more people who bought policies, kept them for years and then canceled them, which would create profit for the carrier; however, time has proven that policy holders maintain long-term care more so than any other type of policy. So take time to compare. Listed below are some important considerations.

- Is the plan tax-qualified? If so, you may be able to deduct all or part of the LTC premiums when you file your federal income tax. Also, benefits paid are generally exempt from taxes. (Consult your tax advisor.)
- Does the LTC policy pay benefits by the expense-incurred method, indemnity method or disability method? Which method is best for you?
- Will the policy pay benefits to family members who provide in-home care?
- How does the policy define the facilities that qualify for LTC benefits? How does it define "assisted living facility"?
- How does the "maximum lifetime benefit" compare to other policies?

After reading these questions, you probably realize that you don't want to buy your LTC insurance from the first Tom, Dick or Harry who offers you a policy. There were more than 80 companies at one time offering coverage, but now that number is down to about five that have been able to make it in this product line. LTC insurance should complement your entire retirement plan to protect your assets. It's something that can be custom fitted to your needs — so talk it over with a professional who has taken the time to get to know you. Long-term care insurance is not for everyone. High net-worth or large fixed income earners from pensions and annuities can make it unnecessary to purchase LTC insurance. On the flip side, too little in cash assets to protect is not a good choice, either. In fact, there are suitability regulations that producers and carriers have a legal responsibility to comply with.

## Cost of LTC Insurance

As you may already suspect, the younger and healthier you are when you purchase your LTC insurance, the cheaper it is. Just so you know, the average age for buying LTC is 57. We will illustrate the reason why by taking a look at an individual and couples aged 55, 60 and 65, all rated as "preferred health." The chart below was provided by the 2012 LTC Insurance Price Index, and it gives us a pretty good idea of costs. I am so thankful I chose to buy my policy when I was 30; I have paid for a longer time, but I have also locked in my costs.

*Calculations are based on: $150 daily benefit, 3-year benefit period, 90-day elimination period, 100 percent home care benefit and 3 percent inflation compounded annually. Includes spousal discount (where applicable). Keep in mind that these are examples only and your actual costs will vary by company, product, your age, health and other factors.*

| Age | Monthly Cost | Immediate Value | Value at Age 80 | Value at Age 85 |
|---|---|---|---|---|
| 55 (single) | $144 | $170,000 | $354,000 | $418,000 |
| 55 (couple) | $225 | $340,000 | $708,000 | $836,000 |
| 60 (couple) | $278 | $340,000 | $611,000 | $708,000 |
| 65 (couple) | $369 | $340,000 | $533,000 | $611,000 |

Traditional long-term care insurance is a "use it or lose it" proposition. You could pay expensive premiums for 30 years and "die with your boots on," never needing the care. Those premium dollars are gone forever. It's like paying car insurance premiums and never having an accident. Some people may balk at the idea of paying for insurance that they may never use, but when are you going to know that? You won't! Not until your journey here has ended, and at that point, you won't care. Besides that, who are you really buying the LTC insurance for, anyway? Husbands don't buy it for themselves. They buy it so that IF they need long-term care, they won't drain the bank and leave their spouse penniless for the next 20 or 30 years that she may have ahead of her. Wives buy it to protect their husbands. In my profession, we call that asset protection. Here's another way to look at it: Would you rather write checks for $150 to $200 a month to purchase protection or checks for $4,000 to $6,000 each month to pay for nursing home care?

For those who want traditional LTC insurance and were declined due to health issues, it might be worthwhile to reapply. If three to five years have passed and you've recovered, the health issue might be considered resolved. If that's the case, there's a pretty good chance that you can qualify.

## Self-Insure

Some people have plenty of assets and are tempted to self-insure. However, I'd like to suggest that they have their cake and eat it too. If you have $300,000 set aside for LTC, as some gurus suggest, and you are still in good health, why not use part of the profits from that investment to purchase LTC insurance? For example, if you earn 5 percent annually on $300,000 for a profit of $15,000 a year, why not redirect $3,336 of that profit each year to pay LTC insurance premiums? (See previous chart for couple aged 60.) This will let you leave a legacy to your loved ones, instead of giving it to the nursing home.

## Life Insurance With a LTC Rider

Life insurance with a LTC rider is a great option for naysayers who don't want to throw money down the drain if they do not use the policy, but still want to protect their assets with the death benefit that life insurance offers. You could reposition some assets into a single pay policy or make periodic premium payments. According to LongTermCare.gov, you have about a three out of four chance of needing the LTC portion of the policy. But if you *don't* use that portion, you still have the opportunity to pass a nice legacy on to your beneficiaries. These plans can also be "tax qualified," so be sure to talk to your retirement planner and your tax planner to see if this is the best option for you.

## Annuity With a LTC Rider

Some people who want LTC insurance simply cannot qualify, while others want to create an income stream and have plenty of assets. Maybe they have or had cancer, diabetes or a stroke. In these scenarios, an annuity with a LTC rider could be a good option. It's also a viable option for the naysayer. Let's say that a couple puts $100,000 into an annuity with a two-year, 7 percent rollup. In two years, they will have $114,000. The payout is about 5 percent per year, or around $5,500. Now let's say that the husband needs long-term care. Immediately, the rider kicks in and he receives $11,000 a year. At the end of five years, he passes away. His wife still receives $5,500 a year for the rest of her life. Some policies have the ability to discontinue the policy or take the monies over a short period to pay the costs as well.

## Have a Family Meeting

Talking to adult children about your LTC preferences and planning can be awkward, to say the least. I'd go so far as to say that you'd have to have a lot of courage to broach the subject. But, the dividends that it will pay down the line are priceless. If we brought your children into a room and asked them if you should get LTC insurance, I hope they would say, "No, Mom and Dad, we will take care of you!" But reality sets in when you're not in the room anymore and the questions of who can afford to quit their job to perform care, could they still send the kids to college among many other factors become the topic of conversation because of this choice. Children typically want to please their parents, but with no real information to go by, they may have conflicting ideas about what your ideal care looks like. For instance, some children envision moving Mom and Dad in with them. But sometimes Mom and Dad don't want to live with their adult children. Perhaps it is for several reasons, too. Maybe they don't want to be a burden, especially if they have dementia. Or maybe they would genuinely prefer a retirement community filled with people their own age and with shared interests.

There has been a revolution of sorts in the area of long-term care facilities, and families really need to explore this aspect of late life. Traditional nursing homes are still around, but there are many more retirement communities opening with a variety of care options available. Arising from this change movement, adult day care centers are becoming more popular because they allow people to remain in their homes longer by bringing them to caregiving facilities for several hours a day. Other creative care options continue to evolve for those who remain at home. Why not take some family field trips to check out the possibilities in your area? Make it fun. You'll likely be amazed at what is out there. At the same time, make sure you tell your adult children about your insurances and the plans you've put in place. Approaching the topic of long-term care before a crisis arises is like giving your family more ballast for encroaching stormy seas.

---

# Medicaid

We all have a backup plan, also known as the government's plan. It's called Medicaid. If you truly can't afford a nursing home and need one, Medicaid will pay for it. The big downside is that you have to "spend down" your income and assets until you are eligible. Without a LTC plan, the "spend down" might be a lot easier than you think. In fact, the American Association for Long-Term Care made this sobering prediction: "Many boomers will fall so far into poverty that they will eventually qualify for Medicaid." That sounds like a dire prediction on the face of it, but there is valid evidence for such a prediction. Would it surprise you to know that 50 percent of the care given to those in nursing homes is paid for through Medicaid and that 97 percent of Americans have no long-term care protection?

Medicaid is a government provision and a Godsend for many people. Before the 19th century, people who could not afford long-term care and who did not have family to care for them were at the mercy of the almshouses (poorhouses). People in these long-term care institutions were literally called "inmates," were forced to wear special uniforms and were often subject to the horrors of abandonment, disgrace, humiliation and neglect. Adding to the trauma was the common practice of placing older adults alongside the mentally insane, the inebriated and the homeless.

Even after the passage of Medicare and Medicaid in 1965, many nursing homes doled out substandard care and were nicknamed "warehouses" or "junkyards" for the aged. It wasn't until 1971 that federal regulations began and enforcement standards for long-term care facilities ensued. Later laws established a single set of rules for facilities hoping to receive Medicaid funds and provided a safe avenue for residents and their families to voice complaints against care facilities. This trickle-down effect has transformed the long-term care industry and even spurred the evolution of LTC insurance options. Today, a growing number of nursing homes provide excellent care. They are not the nursing homes of our ancestors or even of our grandparents. Largely, we have Medicaid to thank.

---

# Medicare and Medigap

Long-term care isn't the only cost that can erode our assets. Our nest egg needs protection from the onslaught of illness and injury. Once we turn 65 and enroll, Medicare takes care of a good portion of our medical expenses.

For the history buffs, we have President Lyndon B. Johnson to thank for that. On July 30, 1965, he signed an amendment to the Social Security Act, making government-funded health insurance available to virtually all U.S. citizens aged 65 and older. This was especially good for the 35 percent of the 65-and-over population who were uninsured. Soon after, an interesting trend began to appear. With better health care, people started living longer. This, of course, contributed to the growing LTC dilemma, but it also sparked new scientific research to help aging adults enjoy a better quality of life. Science is remarkable, but it is not without cost. In time, there came to be significant gaps between what science could provide and what the "original Medicare" would cover. Some of these gaps include co-payments (usually a set dollar amount such as $10 for a doctor's visit), co-insurance (usually a percentage after you pay your deductible, such as 20 percent) and your deductible (the amount you must pay before Medicare or other insurances pay). To fill in the gaps, two solutions were created. First, though, let's take a brief look at different parts of Medicare.

**PART A**
- Inpatient care ( hospitals)
- Skilled care (nursing facility, hospice and home health care)

**PART B**
- Doctors' visits and other health care providers' services, outpatient hospital care, durable medical equipment and home health care
- Preventive care to help maintain your health and manage illnesses

**PART C - Medicare Advantage Plan**
- Includes everything covered under Part A and Part B
- Administered by Medicare-approved private insurance companies

- Usually includes Part D as part of the plan
- May include optional benefits and services for additional cost

**PART D**

- Helps pay for outpatient prescription drugs
- Administered by Medicare-approved private insurance companies
- Designed to lower prescription drug costs and help protect against rising costs

Essentially, you have two ways to get your Medicare coverage. You can choose the original Medicare or a Medicare Advantage Plan. If you choose a Medicare Advantage Plan, you are choosing a "built in" gap protection plan. Basically, it operates like an HMO (health maintenance organization) or PPO (preferred provider organization). You limit your care to authorized providers in a network for the trade-off of lower coverage costs. This option works great for plenty of people, and it negates the need to buy an additional Medigap policy. In fact, you *can't* purchase a Medigap policy if you choose a Medicare Advantage Plan; it duplicates coverage.

Advantage plans are offered by private insurers; premiums and availability vary depending on the county in which you live. In some areas, these work like a charm. Medical facilities and doctors in the network are numerous and the monthly premiums for the plans can be extremely low — even zero in some cases. In other areas, however, they may not be a viable option. Those who want to make sure they have all options available to them when it comes to their medical care and wish to have complete coverage will usually opt for a Medigap policy, also referred to as a Medicare supplement. Even though the cost for a Medigap policy may average $150 per month or more, the coverage is not restricted to a network. When combined with the original Medicare, the resulting coverage is quite comprehensive. There are several plans available within this strategy, so there is no reason for anyone to go without medical insurance once they turn 65.

Regardless of whether you choose a Medicare Advantage plan path or a Medigap (Medicare Supplement) plan path, it is important that you work with an expert who is a broker and can give an unbiased review of your options. Make sure that you discuss with your expert any actions you have already taken regarding Medicare. Some actions may limit choices. For example, once we were working with a couple who had recently moved from another state. They neglected to mention that they had already signed up for a new prescription drug plan upon setting up residence in our state. Doing so used their special election period, thus preventing them from being able to make a selection with us.

## Medigap Open Enrollment Period

Generally, you have one chance to get your lowest possible cost on a guaranteed renewable Medigap policy, regardless of your past or present health. Because Medicare, a government-run program, is involved, Uncle Sam dictates when and how you may enroll. You have a specified window of time in which to apply for this type of coverage. Open enrollment is one of the rare freebies in life. The playing field, or maybe I should call it the "paying" field, is leveled and it's a great asset protector. If you are a candidate for this type of coverage, I recommend that you know when your personal open enrollment period begins and ends and mark it on your calendar in big fat red letters! This is a one-time-only window, and you want to make sure that you use it.

Your six-month open enrollment period begins in the first month that you are 65 years old AND you are covered under Medicare Part B. (You must meet both of these requirements to purchase Medigap.) During this six-month period, federal law protects you from being denied coverage or charged higher rates due to past or present health problems. Some individuals choose to remain on work coverage past turning 65 and delay Part B enrollment. In those cases, open enrollment occurs when you enroll in Part B. The other exception to enrolling at age 65 is when an individual is on Social Security disability for 24 consecutive months, then regardless of age, they become eligible for A and B of Medicare after meeting that requirement.

Why do you need six months? Well, there are several plans out there and many different insurance companies offer them. You will likely need time to shop for the one most suitable for you. The federal government has made it easy to compare plans because all Medigap policies are standardized and assigned a letter A through N. So if you compare two policies sold with the same letter (Plan A with Plan A), the only difference will be the cost and the name of the insurance carrier. Cost can vary considerably, so take time to shop!

---

## Know What You Are Buying

Even though the policy benefits are standardized for policies assigned the same letter, each insurance company is allowed to choose how it will calculate the premiums. These different pricing policies affect your premiums at the time your policy is issued as well as in the future. Community-rated or "no-age-rated" policies charge everyone who has the same Medigap policy the same rate. That means a 65-year-old and a 78-year-old will pay the same rate. Because the premium is not age-based, inflation would be the main factor that would cause a future rise in premiums. Issue-age-rated or "entry-age-rated" policies base the premium on the age you are when you purchase your insurance. The younger you are, the lower your premium. Here too, because future premiums are not based on your current age, the main factor for premium increases would be inflation. Attained-age-rated policies base the premium on your "current" age, so as you may have guessed, your premiums go up as you get older. Premiums can also increase due to inflation. Believe it or not, there is no one, best option for everyone. Each one of these options serves a segment of the population or it wouldn't be offered. By the way, be sure to ask for the list of discounts. Most companies offer discounts for women, nonsmokers, married couples or other qualifiers. You'll also want to take a close look at the deductible versus premium, as this factor may help guide your decision.

Ultimately with health and personal care insurances — LTC, Medicare, Medicaid, Medigap — it is all about getting the care you need while protecting your assets. This is not a time to go it alone. Talk with a qualified retirement planner who has experience with these insurances so that together you can make a plan that best suits your individual retirement needs.

CHAPTER **6**

# Coloring Your Money

I like to keep my workshops fun, so I ask this question early in the program: "What two colors do you think of when you think of a yield sign?" Within a couple of seconds, someone will volunteer, "Yellow and black." The rest nod in agreement. To confirm their answer, I'll display on the screen a photograph of a yellow-and-black yield sign. "Like this?" I ask, and they all agree. Then I show them a picture of a red-and-white yield sign, which is the correct answer; the colors were changed from yellow and black to red and white in 1972! "Oh, that's right!" someone in the audience will say, "They DID change the colors, didn't they?"

The triangular yield sign with the word "YIELD" in black capital letters on a background of yellow was introduced in 1950, and it was what young drivers of that era grew up with. Yield signs after 1972 kept the inverted triangle but put a thick red border around the edges, keeping a smaller, white triangle in the center with the word "YIELD" in red capital letters. As I am writing, this change occurred 42 years ago, and we are still seeing the sign the way it used to be instead of how it appears now. Why is that? I'm not sure I know, but it does go to show that we are all ignorant to certain changes. What I wondered was why the highway people changed the sign! What was wrong with the old one?

As it turns out, the old yield sign did work fine for Americans but not so well for visitors from other countries. Many visitors couldn't understand the word "yield" and also misunderstood the shape and color of the sign to mean "stop." Therefore, the Federal Highway Administration got with the beat and adopted the standardized European yield sign, which we see today, and in effect adopted universal traffic sign language. The new standardized shape and color

79

meant that world travelers would recognize a yield sign whether the words on the face said "yield," "ceda el paso" or even if the sign had no words. This made the streets of America safer for everyone.

## How Do You See Your Retirement Plan?

Like the yield sign, we don't always see our retirement plan for what it is — we see it as it used to be. For the first 30 or so years of our working life, the purpose of our retirement account is to **grow money** for our golden years. Once we near retirement, the purpose changes because our needs change. Once we retire, we need a paycheck that will last us for the rest of our lives. If we are not careful, we can begin to believe that the growth investments that got us *to* retirement are still suitable vehicles to get us *through* retirement, and it is simply not the case.

Let me share a real life example: Mike and Sharon (not their real names) first visited our office to buy Medigap insurance policies. They had turned 65 and wanted something that would pick up where their Medicare coverage left off. In our office, we have specialists who work with nothing but Medicare and supplemental health coverage for seniors. I struck up a conversation with the couple as they were leaving and invited them to attend one of my educational retirement workshops. They told me it would be a waste of time, because they had been with their current advisor for 15 years and couldn't imagine making a change. I told them I admired that kind of loyalty but the invitation still stood. If nothing else, they could give me some feedback on what they thought about the program. So that time came... What they heard piqued their interest enough that they asked me to give them a second opinion on their retirement plan.

What Mike and Sharon had in place was a complex portfolio comprising stocks, bonds, mutual funds and other investments. At that moment, they had $552,000 in assets. I say "at that moment" because, as we all know, these types of investments are capable of fluctuating dramatically. Their strategy was to withdraw $2,000 per month from their investments to fill the gap between their Social Security and Mike's pension plan.

When I showed them a projection, based on historical market returns, it was clear that they were on track to run out of money somewhere in their mid-80s. I still remember the shocked look in their eyes. It was a real wake-up call for them. They began to realize that they didn't have quite the retirement vehicle that they thought they had.

Instead of getting all complicated, I used the **universal language of red money and green money** to explain their options.

---

## Red Money — Green Money

**Red Money is risk money.** We are willing to expose our Red Money to market risk in hopes of greater gains. Because of that, some people also call it their "I hope so" money. Red Money investments require time — usually 10 years or longer — to be effective, and there are no guarantees. They're a popular choice for young investors because time is on their side to have nothing but Red Money on the table. It's also common for the mega-wealthy to allow Red Money to dominate their portfolios because they can afford to lose money. As Arnold Schwarzenegger put it, "Money doesn't make you happy. I now have $50 million, but I was just as happy when I had $48 million."

One of the best questions to ask yourself when contemplating a Red Money investment is, "If I were to lose some or all of this money, would I be upset?" If the answer is yes, then a Green Money investment could be a better match for you.

**Green Money is guaranteed money.** Green Money is all about protection and guarantees. Green Money may get a lower rate of return, but we are willing to trade that for the security of knowing that it will still be there when we look for it. With Green Money, we may have a locked interest rate, which is predictable and declared. As a general rule, the older we get, the more we shift our assets to Green Money.

**Green Money products include:**

- Checking
- Savings
- CDs (certificates of deposit)

- Money markets
- Fixed annuities

Each of these investments is guaranteed. The FDIC insures the first four categories as long as they are purchased through a bank. Fixed annuities and fixed index annuities are backed by the financial strength of the carrying insurance company. What is it that checking, savings, money market accounts and certificates of deposit have in common? They have low interest rates or no interest rate at all, but the principal is guaranteed. At the time of this writing, interest rates on CDs are at an all-time low. They have earned some dubious nicknames, such as "certificates of disappointment," and "constantly dropping" accounts. But at least the rates of interest they do earn are usually fixed and the principal is guaranteed.

**Red Money products include:**
- Individual stocks
- Individual bonds
- Mutual funds
- ETFs (exchange traded funds)
- REITs (real estate investment trusts)
- Variable annuities
- Precious metals and energy

All Red Money investments contain risk. After what happened to the stock market in 2008, I probably don't have to get on a soapbox to convince anyone that individual stocks or mutual funds carry risk. Some beg to differ on **bonds**, however. At first glance, you might think that bonds (corporate, municipal or high yield) belong in the Green Money category. After all, bonds have a defined rate of return and a maturity date. However, between the purchase date and the maturity date, bond prices can fluctuate with similar volatility to stocks. With interest rate risk and longevity risk, the general rule of thumb is that when interest rates go up, bond prices go down. **ETFs** (exchange traded funds) are like mutual funds that trade on the stock market. Most of them are tied to a market index, so even though they are more liquid than mutual funds, they are still Red

Money investments. The same goes for **REITs** (real estate investment trusts). **Variable annuities** are very different from traditional, fixed or indexed annuities. In variable annuities, your principal is at risk because you are investing in sub-accounts that operate like mutual funds. If you have a variable annuity, I recommend that you have a professional retirement planner take a second look — if only to clarify how it operates. These are the products that tend to give the annuity industry a bad name because of the high fees. Last on the list, **precious metals, energy** and other commodities are subject to market fluctuations and liquidity risks.

**Yellow Money**, a third color, would fall somewhere on the financial product spectrum between Green and Red Money. Yellow Money products are generally considered conservative because they offer principal protection, but they also provide the opportunity for greater interest credits. A good example might be a fixed index annuity with interest credits that are linked to the performance of a market index but are never actually invested in the market. In years where the index performance is positive, the fixed index annuity is credited with interest up to a predetermined cap. In years when the index performance is negative, the annuity receives no interest credits *but* it will not lose any of the interest credits from previous years. Indexed CDs, or market-linked CDs, are a relatively new addition on the banking scene. These new variations on an old theme work similarly to a fixed index annuity. With both indexed CDs and fixed index annuities, you will pay a penalty if you withdraw your funds early. As with any financial vehicle, you will want to fully understand all of the product's restrictions and limitations before making a purchasing decision.

**Yellow Money products include:**
- Fixed index annuities
- Indexed CDs

So how did Mike and Sharon's $550,000 portfolio stack up? Without getting too bogged down in the details, Mike and Sharon quickly realized that about 80 percent of their retirement money was Red Money. This is almost polar opposite of what the Rule of 100 would recommend.

**The Rule of 100** is an investing guideline that calls for investing according to your age. Take the number 100, subtract your age and put a percent sign after it. That is the percentage of your money you should have in at-risk investments. You should keep the rest safe. Additionally, I believe that one can account for risk tolerance in addition to the "Rule of 100". Take your risk number created from the traditional Rule of 100 and, in the case of a conservative investor, subtract an additional 20 percent. For the aggressive investor, add 20 percent. This then accounts for all three types of risk tolerance in adherence with the rule; granted this is not a hard and fast actual rule, but rather is a guideline to help you make a determination based on your own factors.

In the case of Mike and Sharon, they could see that if they left things the way they were, they stood a good chance of running out of money in their mid-80s. One of the points they had gleaned from the workshop they had just attended was that Americans are living longer. They learned that, as a couple, there was a 50/50 chance that one of them would live to be 92.

With our trademarked Round Table Retirement Process, I showed them how they could receive a guaranteed income, not only through their 80s, but for the rest of their lives. This is guaranteed by the claims-paying ability of the A-rated insurance carriers we utilized; however, that was guarantee enough for them.

"Can you do this?" they asked.

"The numbers are right here," I replied.

They looked at the paper, then looked at each other, and then looked at me and said, "Do it."

Now, here is the cool thing. They told me that before they came to see me, they knew their money was at risk but said they really didn't know what else they could do. They kept thinking about the "what ifs." What if inflation picks up? What if we need long-term care? What if one of us lives to be 95? Therefore, they couldn't really enjoy their retirement because they felt as though they had to squeeze every nickel while bracing themselves for the worst. What a dark shadow this cast on their golden years. When we began to systematically address one issue after another, it was as if the sun broke through the clouds. As a retirement planner, one of the greatest rewards is knowing I have helped people stride boldly into retirement.

## Taxes, Fees, Commissions and Inflation

Market volatility is not the only risk for investors. A risk is anything that gets between you and your money. Four "bandits" we have to watch out for are taxes, fees, commissions and inflation.

We will never get rid of taxes as long as we live in a democratic society. But if we have a choice between tax-deferred and taxable, we gravitate toward the tax-deferred. The benefit for us is that we could be in a lower tax bracket after retirement, and if we are, tax deferral could save us money. The benefit for Uncle Sam is that retirees will still be feeding the machine even as the ratio of workers to retirees continues to diminish. However, this strategy only works until we are 70.

When it comes to fees and commission, I am not saying that retirement planners should work for free. After all, it's hard work keeping up with the latest tax laws, products and market trends. Nevertheless, as an investor, you should know exactly what you're paying in fees and commissions. That means it's up to you to ask and then to see it in writing. In fact, losing too much money to commissions is one of the top five reasons that investors make low returns even when the stock market is climbing. According to Dalbar, an independent research firm, people who invest in the stock market buy and sell too often. Each time you buy and each time you sell, you pay a commission, which reduces your net profits. Mutual fund management fees can vary considerably. Inflation is especially sneaky. If you are making 5 percent on an investment, but the rate of inflation is 2 percent, then you are really only netting 3 percent. Worse yet, if you have your money in a 2 percent CD and inflation is 2 percent, you're not making any money at all!

## Risk of Waiting

Before the last market crash, there were some investors who sensed that the membrane on the housing bubble was stretching too thin and that something had to give. Those who acted on that "hunch" and removed their money from the stock market in 2007 probably avoided losing half their fortune. Those few converted their holdings into cash and waited for something more trustworthy to come along in which they could more safely invest. However, just how safe was their money when it was sitting in cash? By the time we pay taxes on the paltry yield that high liquidity same-as-cash accounts offer, and by the time inflation takes out its bite, you are going backward.

## Discipline

Regardless of the types of investments you choose, all investing requires discipline. This is especially true if you decide to allocate some of your funds into Red Money investments. Again, Red Money is risk money that you want to leave alone for at least 10 years — or once your income (paycheck) and vacation funds (playcheck) are allocated, you can afford the risk and you can take advantage of the true potential of the market. Resist the temptation to nervously micromanage, change the mix and time the market. It kind of reminds me of the first time I decided to make a cake. I was a teenager and I had no baking experience. There was no way I could make one from scratch. But I figured I could follow the directions on the back of cake mix box, so I gave it a go. I managed to add the oil, eggs and milk and then get it into a pan, just like the directions said. However, instead of setting the timer and leaving it alone, I kept opening the oven door to check on my work. Needless to say, the cake didn't rise properly and the project was a failure. But I felt I had to eat it anyway, and I did!

With investments, eating your mistakes may not be a pleasant experience. The point is this: Pick your Red Money investments carefully by considering all the possible taxes, fees and commissions, then let it grow. You might need to make periodic changes, but if you have really done your homework, then let *time* do its work!

## Know Your Professional

One more thing: Know your professional. Not all financial professionals have access to the same tools. Some are limited to only Red Money products. All they can propose to you are securities that come with risk. Yellow and

Green Money products are not in their bag of tools. If you ask them about Green or Yellow Money products, they are not likely to recommend them for obvious reasons. On the opposite side of the coin, there are some professionals who can only offer insurance products. They are not likely to recommend anything but what they can make a commission on. They aren't licensed to discuss market investments, regardless of the role those investments might play in your overall portfolio. The *best* financial professionals will lay out all the possible options available to you and let you make your own decisions. They also take into account best-case AND worst-case scenarios to tailor a plan to suit your individual needs. It's like trying to put a puzzle together without looking at the box. I feel you must learn what a client needs and wants, then take that blueprint and build the plan to suit. I firmly believe that the right plan, executed at the right time and for the right reasons, can truly enable you to make the most out of your retirement.

In my practice, we bring this full circle by the analogy of a house, with the roof being the most vulnerable part. Just like hail, wind and rain can damage your roof on your fiscal house, the money in the stock market is where the most risk lies. The walls of the house are where we position structure or income production, and the foundation is where we have stability and safety.

**YOUR FISCAL DREAM HOUSE**

## ROOF

Stocks, Funds, Private Equity,
Variable Annuities, Futures, Commodities, etc.

## WALLS

Fixed Income, Index Annuity,
Secured Flexible Income, Hard assets,
Entitlements, Pensions, Not in Market,
Cash-Flow, Inflation Protection, Emergency Funds

## FOUNDATION

CD's, Fixed Annuities, Government Bonds

In this portfolio analogy, the roof is made of higher-risk investments, the walls comprise middle-risk products and the foundation is composed of guaranteed products.

# CHAPTER 7

# The (Retirement) Wheel of Life

The wheel pictured on the next page is a staple at Retirement Solutions Group, Inc. The wheel is my brainchild and one of my proudest creations. It visually expresses the events that take place when we transition from our working years to retirement and how retirement has evolved over the years. The Retirement Wheel began as one of those "noodle doodles" on a desk blotter as I was ruminating on how there has been both an evolution and a revolution when it comes to retirement. The artwork in the wheel aptly pictures how things were and how they have changed. The wheel and the explanation that go along with it help explain how and why this evolution of retirement has taken place — from the pension oriented system of our parents to the 401(k) dominated landscape of today. Currently the baby boomers are retiring at a rate of 10,000 per day. They will be pulling money out of the market at alarming rates to supplement their retirement. In addition, many of them will be forced to withdraw money from their qualified funds — 401(k)s, 403(b)s, IRAs and the like) in the form of Required Minimum Distributions (RMDs) when they reach age 70 ½.

People are creatures of habit. We tend to resist change. Although most folks are aware of the old investing axiom, "buy low, sell high," at some point the inherent risks of the stock market may no longer be acceptable. My point is that things change. This world is different from the one in which we grew up. Retirees must understand this if they are to enjoy a retirement free of financial worries. They need to understand concepts such as income planning, legacy planning and conserving principal.

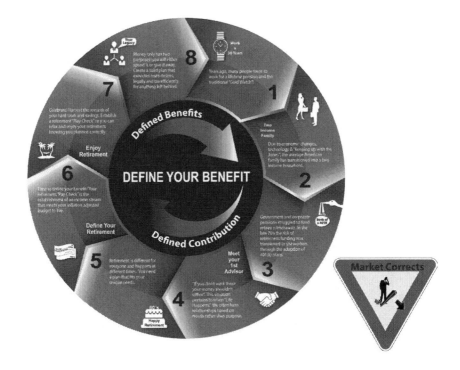

## 1.  The Pension and the Gold Watch

Prior to World War II, life was simpler. Typically, men went to work while their wives stayed home to tend to the children. Employers placed a value on loyalty and long years of service. They provided defined benefit pension plans for their workers that guaranteed them a portion of their salary after they retired for as long as they lived. The company funded the pension plan. All the employees had to do was show up for work every day and after 30 or so years of loyal service, they could count on a gold watch and a paycheck for the rest of their lives. If we were to compare this to a football scenario, it was as if the company was running the offense and the defense of the retirement plan. No matter what, you were guaranteed "x" amount of dollars every month for the rest of your life. Believe it or not, at that time a couple could retire comfortably on the husband's pension checks. Eighty-eight percent of people today do not have defined benefit plans and if they do, they typically don't cover enough.

## 2. The Two-Income Family

World War II was a pivotal period for family dynamics. With so many men headed to combat overseas, America needed more workers. To fill the need, Uncle Sam conjured up what is now called the most successful recruitment campaign in U.S. history. Remember *Rosie the Riveter?* She was the star of the "We can do it" campaign. Using posters, media and even a

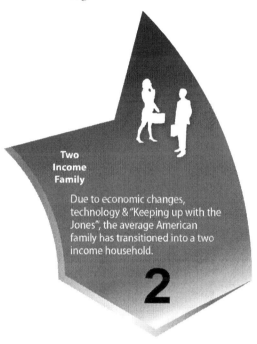

Two Income Family

Due to economic changes, technology & "Keeping up with the Jones", the average American family has transitioned into a two income household.

2

song, working women were heralded as being patriotic and efficient without having to sacrifice beauty. The first group to fall under the marketing spell was women who were already working. They were encouraged to trade in low paying jobs for better paying factory work in war production plants. Even though a woman was doing the same job as a man had previously, she was paid 65 percent less. Yet, she was still bringing home more bacon than she did in non-factory work.

More workers were needed, so the next leg of the campaign targeted young girls who had barely graduated high school. When that, too, fell far short, married women with children were called upon. The problem was most of them in this category didn't want to work and didn't have to work. Therefore, the government used a persuasive blend of pride and fear to lure the group into the workplace. Women were told the war would end sooner if they filled the vacant factory jobs. At the same time, it was implied that more soldiers would die if married women refused to make the needed munitions and supplies. American illustrator Norman Rockwell immortalized Rosie the Riveter on the May 29, 1943 (Memorial Day) cover of the Saturday Evening Post. The painting was the first visual image to incorporate the 'Rosie' name and portrayed a proud, muscular young woman on her lunch break; with a glorious red, white, and blue American flag for a backdrop. The red-haired Rosie, dressed in coveralls, munches on her sandwich with a rivet gun across her lap. Oddly, Rockwell has her wearing penny loafers and bright red socks. Her insouciant expression seems to say, "I can do the job as well as any man." After the war ended, the iconic Rosie became the image of choice in the fight to broaden women's civil rights. The "We Can Do It!" campaign drew over 6 million previously non-employed women into the workforce and forever changed the dynamics of the American family. After the war, some women returned to their roles as wives and mothers, but others wanted to keep their jobs. The 1950s became a transitional time, but clearly, the seeds had been sown for two-income families. As I write this, women compose 47 percent of the American workforce.

At the same time as the "Rosie" campaign, we began changing the way we think about money. Prior to 1950, there really weren't that many luxuries to buy. When people did make a purchase, they typically paid cash. After 1950, however, Americans couldn't get enough. Luxuries became necessities and America became the land of plenty filled with automatic clothes washers and dryers, automatic dishwashers, microwave ovens, color televisions, computers, video games, cellphones and a seemingly never ending evolution of iPhones, iPads, iPods, tablets and more. Somewhere along the line, most Americans stopped paying cash for all these goodies and went with the buy-now-pay-later option. Credit cards became increasingly easy to obtain and families started taking on more debt. On the plus side, buying on credit built the United States into the economic giant that it is today. However, on the minus side, even two-income households soon found themselves saddled with oppressive debt, with couples struggling to pay off high-interest loans while they attempted to save for their future. This served to complicate planning for retirement. It was very simple in the "Leave it to Beaver" days when only the husband worked and his pension was all that was necessary for security in retirement. Now that we have to keep up with the Joneses and put all the kids through school, a two-income household is almost a must.

### 3.   Birth of the 401(k)

Company-sponsored defined benefit pension plans worked well for many years. Then some companies started promising more than they could pay. A turning point occurred in 1963, when Studebaker Corporation — an automobile manufacturing company — closed its plant and failed to keep its pension promises. For some reason, the U.S. buying public had fallen out of love with the futuristic car and Studebaker couldn't fund its pension programs with money it didn't have. The United Auto Workers union howled in protest and the matter became a topic for the nightly television news. As it turns out, Studebaker was not the only company mishandling its employees' pension plans. Nine years later, NBC had enough grist for the

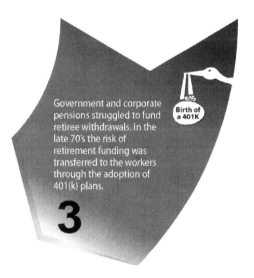

Government and corporate pensions struggled to fund retiree withdrawals. In the late 70's the risk of retirement funding was transferred to the workers through the adoption of 401(k) plans.

**3**

mill to air the documentary titled, "Pensions: The Broken Promise." With the growing problem publicly exposed, Congress held a series of public hearings culminating in the **Employee Retirement Income Security Act of 1974 (ERISA)**. This new law would now protect pension plan participants.

ERISA required companies to openly disclose the value of each participant's pension account and to provide documentation that they were following specific government regulations. It's probably no accident that President Gerald R.

Ford signed this into law on Labor Day — a day dedicated to the American worker.

This new level of accountability and the paperwork it demanded made defined benefit pension plans more cumbersome for employers. However, in less than a decade, the 401(k) subsection of the Internal Revenue Code was used to define a new type of pension plan. Conveniently named after the code, this new plan was a defined *contribution* plan. Employers supported it because now all of the responsibility rested on the employees' shoulders. Sure, employers could (and often did) match employees' contributions to a stated limit, but now it was up to the employees to define how much they would have deducted from their paychecks and how they would invest their savings. These new retirement plans were touted as a win-win for everyone. Employers could support their employees with the matching contribution without taking responsibility for the investment outcomes. At the same time, employees had more control over their investments. Main Street went to Wall Street. At this time, not everyone was versed in the market, but everyone was heading into it. The big switch from defined benefit plans or pensions to defined contribution plans was upon us. The 401(k) plans were portable, too. If you decided to change jobs, you could roll over your 401(k) to another qualified plan or convert it to an individual IRA. Today, company-sponsored defined benefit plans, where the company carries all of the responsibility, are almost extinct. Most companies now offer some form of a defined contribution plan where you, the worker, take all the responsibility. While the 401(k) is the most common plan, there are a few others.

**Here is the way a few of them work:**

**401(k) plans:** You decide, up to a legal limit, how much pretax money you want deducted from your paycheck. You decide how that money will be invested within your plan's available mutual funds and investment options. Your employer may match your contribution up to a certain percentage.

**Profit-sharing plans:** Your employer decides how much stock or cash to contribute to your account based on a stated formula.

**Employee stock ownership plan (ESOP):** Your pretax contributions to this plan are invested primarily in company stock.

**Simplified employee pension plans (SEPs):** An IRA is set up to accept your pretax contributions and your employer's pretax contributions. Because the plan is IRA based, if certain requirements are met, employers are excluded from the reporting requirements of most defined contribution plans.

**Savings incentive match plans for employees of small employers (SIMPLEs):** Companies with 100 or fewer employees can offer either a SIMPLE IRA or SIMPLE 401(k). In each instance, the burden of paperwork is removed from the employer because the employee owns the account and the financial institution accepting the funds provides most of the required documentation. The required employer contributions are immediately 100 percent vested in both plans.

### 4.   Meet Your First Advisor

You'll notice on the Wheel of Retirement that I inserted an extra image between "Birth of a 401(k)" and "Happy Retirement." That's because most of us don't make a change until we have to. Early on,

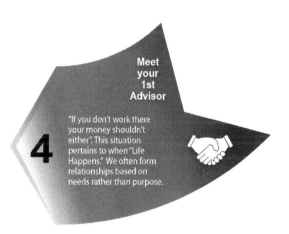

Meet your 1st Advisor

"If you don't work there your money shouldn't either". This situation pertains to when "Life Happens." We often form relationships based on needs rather than purpose.

401(k)s did pretty well — especially during the 1990s when it seemed the market could do no wrong. Many people became complacent and even overconfident. While some looked at their 401(k) statements and smiled, others stopped looking them because they began to take the remarkable growth for granted. Then the market began to change course. In the 2000s, some people's retirement accounts dropped by 50 percent. That was hard-earned money, money needed for retirement, and it was gone. If you were fortunate, you still had time to recoup your losses. If you had already retired and hadn't changed your strategy to a more defensive one before the market fell, you may have found yourself picking up part-time work or lowering your standard of living. In either case, people began seeking out their first personal financial advisors.

Advisors specialize much like doctors or lawyers. When you are young, you go to a pediatrician, and as you get older you go to various specialists for different ailments. Another thing to consider is you wouldn't want to work with a doctor who treats your symptoms without diagnosing the problem first or gives all of his or her patients the same treatment regardless of symptoms. Imagine going to see the doctor for the first time and he or she walks into the room and says you need Prozac. You're an individual and need to be treated as such. Financial planning should be tailored to you, not one size fits all.

Advisors specialize in at least three categories: accumulation, preservation and distribution. My specialty has been in the latter two. Accumulation advisors typically will bellow the phrase "It's only a paper loss!" whenever there is a market correction. But see, if you're getting close to retirement, then time is not on your side. It takes a preservation advisor to help you get through the difficult transition that is retirement.

Over time, many people began to realize that not all financial advisors are created equal. People also began to suspect the advice that got them **to** retirement was not necessarily the same they needed to get them **through** retirement.

### 10 Questions

Here are 10 questions you would do well to ask **before** you hire an investment advisor:

1. **Why did you choose this profession?** Typically, people become advisors for one of three reasons. They love puzzles and investment strategies, they love people and relationships or they have a deeply personal connection to helping others with their financial planning.

2. **What happens if you can't be reached?** Sometimes advisors are sick, on vacation or out of cell range. Is there someone at the office who can handle your transactions in their absence? Will they have knowledge of your plans?

3. **Why should I choose you?** Most advisors are ethical and honest. However, they may have different motivations. If the advisor you are

considering answers this question by focusing on him or herself, that might be a red flag. But if the advisor focuses on you and your needs, it could indicate a sincere interest in doing what is best for you.

4. **Can you describe your ideal client?** Obviously, it is important that you refrain from telling the advisor too much about yourself before you ask this question. The point is, you want to know if the advisor has plenty of experience working with people at your stage of life. The more closely the advisor's description matches your own circumstances, the better your chances for having found a good match.

5. **How do you get paid?** Advisors typically get paid in one of three ways or in a combination of these ways. **Commissions** are paid on some products sold by advisors. Sometimes, you pay the commission, such as when you invest in a loaded mutual fund. Other times, the commission is paid from the profits by the company offering the product, such as with life insurance or annuity products. Advisors who operate with a **fee for advice** don't earn any money on product sales. Instead, you pay them a flat, hourly or percentage fee. One caution, usually it is up to you to track down the investments that you need and these advisors may not be as fully informed on all of your options. Advisors who operate off of a **fee based on a percentage of your assets** specialize in market-linked accounts that let you trade as much as you want for one flat fee. One key to this question is to notice how the advisor answers. Is the advisor forthright? Is the advisor comfortable with this question? Do you feel that you are getting a complete answer? Remember, it's OK and even necessary that your advisor earns a living, but you want to be sure that the way he or she earns a living is compatible with the products that suit your needs. We delve more deeply into this in the next chapter.

6. **What are my other costs, besides your fees?** Hidden fees can reduce your return. Ask your current or prospective advisor which of these fees you are paying: account set up fees, front-end load, management fees, redemption fees, annual maintenance fees, 12b-1 fees and service fees, advertising fees, annual account fees, termination fees, operating expenses, transfer fees, transaction fees and ongoing

mutual fund fees. Consider asking your advisor for a written disclosure of the fees that you are currently paying or will pay if you implement his or her suggested plan.

7. **What is your methodology for investing?** With this question, you are trying to find out if the advisor has a solid philosophy or just a bunch of products. Ask the advisor, "What is your foundational philosophy that guides your investment strategies?" Ask for details, and ask about the advisor's results.

8. **Do you have a clean regulatory record?** While the majority of advisors do, some don't. Your retirement is too important to trust to chance, and it's easy to double-check. Go to www.finra.org/brokercheck to see if any complaints have been filed against the advisor. Then, go to www.adviserinfo.sec.gov and click on "Investment Advisor Search." Lastly, you can look up an insurance advisor by going to your state's department of insurance website.

9. **Ask yourself: Do I understand what the advisor said?** If you don't understand something at this stage of the game, then it likely will not get any better. It could just be a difference in communication styles. Or, it could be a self-promoting style that uses a lot of jargon to try to impress you. Whatever the case, if you don't feel comfortable, understood and cared for by the time you get to this question, you really need to look for a better match. There is an advisor who can speak in the way that you like to listen and who has professional skills and a strong desire to help you personally. You owe it to yourself to find a good match.

10. **Are you a fiduciary?** These two words, fiduciary and suitability, are critical to determining the type of care you receive from your "trusted" financial advisor. Unfortunately, most of the public is unaware that a minority of advisors are held to a fiduciary standard while a majority of them are held to a much lower, suitability standard of care. Currently, only Registered Investment Advisors are required to act in a fiduciary capacity.

### 5. Happy Retirement

The big day has arrived. It's your day to retire! Retirement is different for everyone. You may decide to volunteer, spend time with family, travel or even start a new career. You need to create a retirement that is uniquely your own. Likely, you will not get the defined benefit pension payout (the paycheck for life from a company pension plan), but you may still get a gold watch. As for the paychecks for life, that depends on what you did with your 401(k) and other investments. Remember, for most of us now, it is completely up to us to create an income for life — in other words, define your own benefits. If we start with a budget, move our strategy from offensive (accumulating big gains by taking big risks) to defensive (holding ground and limiting losses or guaranteeing assets by accepting lower returns) and then execute our plan, we can have as happy a retirement as possible.

### 6. Paychecks & Playchecks

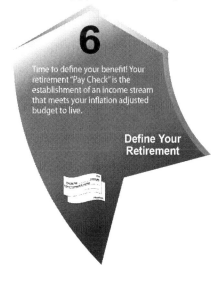

When I consult with people approaching retirement, one of their chief goals is to replace their former workweek paycheck with a regular retirement paycheck. We're funny that way. We like to know that we can depend on a certain amount of money coming in month after month. To accomplish this goal, you should work with a financial professional to figure out how to turn some of your nest egg into a guaranteed monthly income, or "paycheck." This "paycheck" can help fill in the gap between your budget and the income you receive from Social Security and any company sponsored defined benefit plans.

### 7.  Enjoy Retirement

Celebrate! Harvest the rewards of your hard work and savings. Establish a retirement "Play Check" so you can relax and enjoy your retirement knowing you planned correctly.

**Enjoy Retirement**

Once the paycheck is in place, you can use the remainder of your nest egg to fund your playcheck. Playchecks let you do all the things you daydreamed about while you were working hard for 30 years and saving for these golden years. There are a wide variety of investment options for the remaining portion of your nest egg, once the paychecks and playchecks are secured. Retirement can and should be enjoyable. When a well-defined plan is put in place that matches your personal needs, you really can relax. As the proverb recommends, "see good for your hard work." The problem comes in when people skip Step 6 on the Wheel of Retirement. For some reason, people don't always see the need to lock in part of their nest egg with a guaranteed income vehicle. They are afraid that they may be missing an upside advantage that might be on its way. But before long, the market corrects, which it always does, and they then feel even more afraid.

Often, people who delay in securing guaranteed checks come to me feeling anxious. Instead of enjoying a peaceful midday nap in a hammock, like my picture on the wheel suggests, these people are up at all hours of the night calculating and double-checking the effects of the market swings on their nest egg. For most people at this stage of life, the joys of market upswings are not worth the sorrows of market losses. To enjoy retirement, you need to defend the assets you've worked so hard to attain and make sure that you have steady checks you can count on. With today's products, such as fixed index annuities, it's possible to guarantee your principal and income while still earning competitive interest rates. Know that once you are in the last 10 years of your working life, it's time to adopt a progressively defensive strategy that protects your future happiness as a retiree.

## 8. Legacy

We all leave a legacy when we leave this world. What will yours be? Not everyone wants to leave money to his or her heirs. Some people want to spend it all. That's part of their story — their legacy. But I find that most people do want to leave something to their favorite charities and to the next generation. After all, if you look at the Wheel of Retirement, it's our next generation that starts the cycle all over again. By legacy planning, we can actually give our next generation a leg up. But sometimes, and I've witnessed this many times, Uncle Sam ends up getting more of our children's inheritance

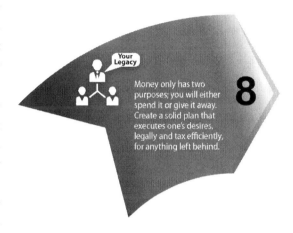

than our heirs do. So now is the time to put the legal and financial programs in place to make sure you are leaving the legacy you intend to leave, and that it is going to the people you intend to leave it to. It always amazes me that even when clients believe they have dotted all the i's and crossed all the t's, our team often finds errors that have been overlooked. The way I see it, your legacy plan is your final hand-off to the next generation. Make it a good one.

## 9. Market Correction

I don't know when the market will correct; my crystal ball is broken. I do, however, feel quite confident that it will at some time. I know that if a correction happens after you pass away, it may affect your family but not you. However, if a correction happens the day after you retire, you may never recover. The preservation years are quite different than the accumulation years in our lives. So yield to reality and protect yourself from inevitability. Proper planning is just that. Money only has two purposes: You will either spend it or give it away, so you might as well enjoy it or your heirs will.

# CHAPTER 8

# Offense and Defense

It is true that soccer (what the rest of the world calls football) is the most popular sport in the world. But when it comes to average attendance per game, American football beats all other sports. The National Football League averages more than 68,000 fans per game. What is it about this American game played with an oddly shaped inflatable oblate spheroid that makes it twice as popular as baseball? Both are team sports, both use balls and both have offense and defense. I think the difference is the speed of the game. Baseball may be the "great American pastime" but to me it seems to be long periods of slow movement interrupted by occasional urgency.

Football is certainly a better metaphor for life. It comes at us hard and fast sometimes, and we can take some hard hits along the way. It makes for a good metaphor for retirement, too. In Chapter 1 of this book, we likened the last few yards of the gridiron just before the goal line to the "red zone" in football, where we need to play conservatively with a keen determination not to fumble the ball by playing fast and loose with our resources, thus preventing us from celebrating a successful, worry-free retirement. A loss in the stock market is still a loss no matter when it comes, but it could have devastating effects if it comes during our transition into retirement.

It is human nature to resist change. Exchanging the known and comfortable position for a new and different one is anathema to most people. We tend to want to keep doing what worked for us in the past, even though our circumstances have changed and now dictate a new direction. In Chapter 6, during our discussion about the color of money, we made the point that the investing strategies that got us *to* retirement may not be the same investing strategy that we need to get us ***through*** retirement.

Once we get to the last 10 years of our working life — our personal red zone — we need investment strategies that defend our nest egg from market loss, inflation and taxes. The best football teams are the ones who have both good ***offense*** and good ***defense***. Your retirement plan might be best if it has a good defense against market downturns (guarantees of principal found in annuities, for example) and a good offense — an investment account to capitalize on market gains. What do you think? Will health care costs, interest rates and taxes go up or down in the future? There is a certain yin and yang to these variables. You cannot do it all in stocks and there are many different types of investment and insurance products available. Whatever the product mix is in your portfolio, the important part is that it meets your risk tolerance and is in line with helping you reach your personal goals. One of the advantages we have as a full-service financial firm is that we can coach both offense and defense, tailoring retirement plans to each individual situation. We work with a careful selection of insurance and investment products for our clients. We research and shop to make sure we offer what we feel best addresses their unique needs.

## Fiduciary vs. Suitability Advice

In the world of financial services, there are essentially two camps: advisors and brokers — both insurance brokers (agents) and investment brokers. The key difference has much to do with the two standards they adhere to — the ***suitability standard*** or the ***fiduciary standard***. If you have never heard of either and you don't understand what the terms mean, you are not alone. A 2011 study by the U.S. Securities and Exchange Commission found that "many investors are also confused by the standards of care that apply to investment advisers and broker-dealers."

The lesser standard is based on suitability. A broker can recommend an investment and an insurance agent can recommend an insurance product if it is "suitable" for your particular age, risk tolerance and investment objectives. If brokers have two or more investments that are "suitable" — two mutual funds that are performing similarly, for example — they can, under the dictates of the suitability standard, recommend the one that pays the highest commission to them. There is nothing illegal or technically unethical about doing that, either. The same would apply for insurance agents with respect to insurance products.

On the other hand, advisors (Investment Advisor Representatives) are bound to the higher fiduciary standard, which requires and legally binds them to offer only what is in the best possible interests of the client, irrespective of any personal gain or reward. The fiduciary standard was established as part of the Investment Advisors Act of 1940 and is regulated by the Securities and Exchange Commission or state securities regulators.

The term "fiduciary" comes from the Latin word "fiducia," meaning "trust." A fiduciary is legally bound to make investment recommendations that are not merely suitable but are in the client's best interest. When there is a conflict of interest, fiduciaries are ethically and legally obligated to put client interests ahead of their own. In some other commercial settings, you pay extra for better service — an upgrade from coach to first class on an airline or a private hospital room, for example — but you pay nothing extra for fiduciary advice. That doesn't mean a fiduciary is not remunerated for his or her services; it just means they are not **motivated** by profit.

So how can you tell if you are working with a fiduciary? Just ask! In fact, let me make it easy for you. Ask this exact question, "Are you acting under the fiduciary standard?" If they say yes, ask them to put it in writing.

I can't stress this enough. Currently, the SEC is pushing to change the law so that every broker and investment adviser representative will have the same standard — the fiduciary standard. In addition, the U.S. Department of Labor has proposed a new law that would force insurance agents to uphold a "best interest" standard when working with qualified retirement plans. Until then, choose wisely. Just so you know, I'm willing to put it in writing. Retirement Solutions Group, Inc. acts under the fiduciary standard. We live our mission statement: "We believe in better."

## How Big Is the Toolbox?

When I was teenager, I had a friend who would do anything to keep his car on the road. Whenever I looked under the hood or under the chassis, I'd see duct tape, shreds of old towels, wire clothes hangers and any number of make-shift fixes for the problems that ailed his rusty chariot. As I look back on it, this friend's ability to make the most out of what he had was downright spellbinding. However, I would not want anyone using that approach to build my retirement plan — yet that is the approach some retirement planners take.

For instance, stockbrokers are typically limited to the tools in their toolbox — stocks, bonds and other market-traded investments — and they tend to make the tool fit the problem. The broker may justify this by claiming that bonds, with a stated rate of interest and a maturity date, qualify as a defensive investment. As we discussed in Chapter 6, because bonds trade on the market and fluctuate like stocks, in some cases they act like "Red Money" or high-risk investments. I can't tell you how many near-retirees walk into my office or attend workshops and tell me that they have 100 percent of their assets exposed to risk in the stock market. This is usually because their brokers are trying to do the best they can with the limited tools available to them. The same goes for those who call themselves retirement planners but only sell insurance products. These planners tend to see life insurance, annuities and other insurance products as the best fix for every offensive and defensive investment in a balanced retirement portfolio.

Years ago, I realized it's better to expand the toolbox instead of forcing the tool to work. It goes back to what being a fiduciary is all about. I wanted to earn the trust that comes from giving my clients the very best choices. So, in 2008, I created RSG Investments Inc. We even have an affiliated relationship with an attorney and a tax firm, but we will delve deeper into probate and legacy planning in the final chapter of this book.

---

## Too Much Defense

Some near-retirees, especially those who experienced the stock market crash of 2008, want to keep their money completely safe. They want to be able to see it and touch it and know that it will not disappear. These investors believe in100 percent liquidity. However, now is not the time to let your money retire to the rocking chair. If your money is not working for you, inflation and taxes will nibble away at your nest egg. In a football scenario, keeping too much of your money liquid is equivalent to letting the opposing team slowly push you backward. Because it happens so gradually, it's not as upsetting as fumbling the ball in a stock market correction. However, either way, you're losing ground.

Just to give you a little perspective, in 2007, a 5-year CD yielded 5.25 percent. That's not too bad. However, in 2012, interest rates fell to their lowest point in 40 years and the rate of return on a 5-year CD plummeted to 1.5 percent. As of the writing of this book, the rate of return for a 5-year CD has bounced up to a whopping 2.25 percent, which is almost on par with inflation. When you take taxes into account, the "safe" investment is actually costing you money. Other options that are about as conservative may offer much better return potential than a 5-year CD. Many times, when the defense (money you cannot afford to lose) is solidly locked in place, funds can be freed up to protect your portfolio from the inroads of inflation. If you find yourself going it alone and your money is sitting on the sidelines, think about meeting with a fiduciary to consider your options. In most cases, initial consultations are free of charge.

## A Balancing Act

I get inspired by watching the best of the best perform, either on stage or in sports. I suppose tightrope walking is an act, not a sport, but it requires supreme physical and mental toughness and nerves of steel — and obviously a great sense of balance. In 2012, 35-year-old Nik Wallenda, a legendary tightrope walker, set his seventh Guinness World Record by crossing Niagara Falls. In 2013, he decided to up the ante by crossing the Grand Canyon, which is seven times higher than Niagara Falls. One slip and he's history. As I watched the feat replayed on TV, the announcer informed viewers that this Wallenda was a seventh-generation member of the famous Flying Wallendas, royalty when it comes to the high wire.

The balance pole that Nik Wallenda chose for the Grand Canyon walk was 30 feet long and weighed 43 pounds! That is quite a hefty weight for a guy who weighs only 198 pounds. As soon as he began his walk, I began to see that this 43-pound pole was not extra weight — it was his lifesaver — literally. Wind gusts pasted his blue shirt to his body and threatened to sweep him off the wire.

Wallenda kept his balance by tilting the pole, sometimes holding it in a nearly vertical position, to counteract the force of the wind.

It is easy for us to lose our balance investment-wise when we experience shifts in the economy such as interest rate changes and stock market volatility. When individual investors go it alone, they usually turn to the stock market with a determination to buy low, sell high and watch their profits grow. The element that usually trips them up is the oldest of foibles — human emotion. Those who are investing with retirement in view are especially vulnerable. The closer they get to retirement, the more heightened their investing emotions may be, causing them to lose their equilibrium.

They may become emotionally attached to a position and feel pressured to stay invested in it regardless of all the "get out now" signals screaming at them from the sidelines. When retirement begins to loom large on the horizon, and fears of not having enough money to retire on begin to surge, emotions may cause the "Las Vegas syndrome" to kick in. They call it "doubling down" at the gambling tables — that is, taking on inordinate risk in an effort to make up for lost time. When market downturns occur, our fears and concerns surface and we end up doing the exact opposite of buying low and selling high.

If the winds of emotion are the force that threatens to knock us off our high wire, we regain our balance through objectivity and professional investing advice offered by a fiduciary whose job it is to track investments and manage portfolios through a wide range of economic weather. The fiduciary's experience, perspective and long-term view can be your balance pole.

# CHAPTER 9

# Drawdown, Distribution & Detour Signs

Have you ever ignored a detour sign? Sometimes you can get away with it, but at other times it can cost you big time.

The following is a true story. It didn't happen to me, but I heard the tale firsthand. It's the night of the high school prom. The young man had just gotten his driver's license but had no car. His date's father felt sorry for the young man and offered to let him drive his daughter to the prom in the family automobile. The loan of the car came with at least an hour of safety instructions, most of which had to do with seatbelts and speed limits. The young man endured the lecture, itching to get behind the wheel. The girl's father should have warned him about detour signs, however, as we shall soon see.

Getting to the prom was no problem. The young man had received clear instructions from the girl's father to have both her and the car home by midnight, whereupon he would drive the young man home. When the youth realized he was running late, he decided to take a shortcut home that he figured would shave about 10 minutes off the trip. It would have, too, if it weren't for the fact that the road was under construction.

The teenager was an inexperienced driver. He saw the signs that said, "Detour Ahead," but he didn't exactly what they meant. Soon, however, he came to a big orange sign that read, "DETOUR, Local Traffic Only" with an arrow pointing toward the alternate route. The road looked just fine to him, however. He reasoned that he was local traffic and continued on his way down the two-lane blacktop, slowly at first, and then picking up speed as his confidence grew. His high-beams illuminated the trouble ahead but he didn't have time to react to it. The road crew had removed a six-foot-long section of pavement, leaving a 2-foot-deep ditch in the middle of the road. The car came to an abrupt halt, its front bumper in the dirt on the other side of the ditch. The kids had their seatbelts fastened and weren't injured, if you don't count the young man's wounded pride. He had to walk to the nearest house and wake up the people inside and asked to use the phone (this was way before cellphones). He then made the painful call to the girl's father, who arranged to have the car, which was not seriously damaged, pulled out of the ditch.

The boy would survive the embarrassment of the incident with a new appreciation for detour signs. As the girl's father needlessly pointed out, the accident could have been avoided had he just paid attention to the detour signs.

## Detour Signs on Retirement Road

Detour signs mean that something up ahead has changed. To get to your destination, you must take a new route. You may have been familiar with the old route, true, but now you must adapt to new road conditions in order to get to where you are going.

The road to retirement has changed in the last few decades. Some of the changes are readily apparent. Pensions have been all but removed from the topography of today's retirement landscape, replaced by 401(k) plans or similar programs that give us more responsibility and control. This was a major game changer. When the Revenue Act of 1978 was passed, the paragraphs under Internal Revenue Code (IRC) Sec. 401(k), for which the plans would eventually be named, went virtually unnoticed. This new provision now allowed employees to defer taxes on a portion of income that they elected to receive as "deferred compensation" instead of direct cash payments. More people became familiar with this new law, however, when it went into effect on Jan. 1, 1980, and it wasn't long before these salary reductions became a source for contributions to defined contribution retirement plans today known as 401(k)s.

Individual retirement accounts were introduced by the Employee Retirement Income Security Act of 1974 (ERISA) and made popular with the Economic Recovery Tax Act of 1981. Roth IRAs were introduced in 1998. Now you could ditch the concept of deferring taxes on the front end and take what many considered to be a better option — getting the taxes out of the way early and receiving the gains from the IRA tax-free upon withdrawal. For some of us, it's better to tax the seed rather than the harvest. To clarify, typically if you will make less money in retirement than when you're working, a traditional IRA will allow the monies potentially to come out in a lower tax bracket than when they entered the account. If, however, the opposite is true and you may be in a higher tax bracket when you retire, a Roth IRA may be attractive because, while you skip taking a tax deduction on the deposits when they go into the account, the growth that accumulates, which you may start withdrawing in retirement, is tax free. When you visit with a fiduciary, he or she can help advise on what's most appropriate in your situation.

If someone on the threshold of their retirement in 1970 could have pulled a Rip Van Winkle and awakened in 2010, he or she would not recognize the modern retirement landscape. Many of the familiar routes to retirement would have detour signs informing the time-traveler that the old routes have significantly changed. Strategies that used to work even as late as the 1990s simply no longer apply. Take, for example, a formula known as "The Four Percent Drawdown Rule."

## The Four Percent Drawdown Rule

In 1994, William Bengen, a California financial advisor and graduate of Massachusetts Institute of Technology who liked to tinker with numbers, came up with something called the "Four Percent Rule," or as some later called it, "The Four Percent Drawdown Rule." Bengen took 60 years of actual stock market returns (not averages) and concluded that retirees could draw down, or withdraw, 4 percent from their active stock market portfolios each year and, by continual rebalancing between stocks and bonds, never run out of money. The idea was pounced upon by stockbrokers, and it soon became gospel among the denizens of Wall Street. Articles in financial magazines hailed it as the solution for retirees who, now that they were statistically living longer, were worried they may outlive their resources.

The problem with the "Four Percent Rule" was that it was developed at a time when the economy was in the middle of one of the longest bull markets in Wall Street history. It wasn't Bengen's fault. He had no way of knowing when the market heyday of the 1990s would end, and that in the next decade investors would experience the bursting of the tech bubble in 2000 and the financial crisis of 2008.

The "Four Percent Rule" allowed for a 4 percent withdrawal of the value of the portfolio each year, including an allowance for inflation. For example, if your portfolio was valued at $250,000, in your first year of retirement you would sell (draw down) $10,000 of your investments for income. The next year, your drawdown would be $10,300 to include a 3 percent increase for inflation. The third year, you would withdraw $10,609. Amazingly, Bengen's research proved that this formula worked during every historical 30-year period for the six-plus decades he analyzed.

In the last few years, however, the warning signs have been popping up left and right in financial periodicals, such as Money and The Wall Street Journal, that what was thought to be the "Holy Grail" of investing just doesn't work anymore. Appearing 20 years after the appearance of the "Four Percent Rule" was an article published in 2014 by Money titled "Forget the 4% Withdrawal Rule," in which Wade Pfau, a professor of retirement income at The American College, lowers Bengen's 4 percent down to just 2.22 percent.

Like Bengen, Pfau produced research from actual market returns as far back as 1926. He pointed out that stocks listed on the S&P 500 index historically average a price-to-earnings ratio of 16. In 2014, Pfau said this average had inflated to 25, adding that without room for growth and upside potential to replenish the drawdowns, the Four Percent Drawdown rule falls apart. In Pfau's estimation, it's not much better in the bond market, which accounts for half the portfolio in a typical drawdown plan. Pfau's research indicates that historically, the 10-year Treasury averages 3.5 percent. However, the yield was only 2.6 percent on the 10-year Treasury in the summer of 2014. Even if yields go up, bondholders will suffer a capital loss because bond prices fall when interest rates rise. This does not bode well for someone who is planning to cash in investments to fund the drawdown. Interestingly, Money magazine went back to William Bengen to see what he thought about Pfau's "detour sign." Bengen said, "I think Pfau has done a great job of looking at the issues. Market valuations are important, and he may be right."

Other headlines and excerpts that spell the end for the "Four Percent Rule" read as follows:

- **4% Rule for Retirement Withdrawals Is Golden No More** ~ New York Times, 2013. "Many financial advisers are rejecting the 4 percent rule as out of touch with present realities."

- **How Much to Withdraw from Retirement Savings** ~ Forbes Magazine, 2013. "When the 4% rule emerged, investment portfolios were earning about 8% annually. Today, they're generally in the 3 to 4% range."

- **Retirees May Need to Rethink 4% Rule** ~ AARP, 2013. "... new research by Morningstar Investment Management suggests that relying on that 4 percent rule of thumb today is risky, thanks to a market in which bond yields and dividends have hovered at record lows for years."

If you are on the road to retirement and there is a bridge out up ahead, you probably want to know about it as soon as possible. If your retirement planner or financial advisor hasn't brought up this new development, you might want to initiate a conversation. It's never a bad idea to get a second opinion. Thirty years from now, you will probably be glad you did. You may even wink at yourself in the mirror, knowing that your younger self took very good care of you way back then.

# Longevity

Something else has changed since the "Four Percent Rule" was conceived — life expectancy. In 1994, the average male could expect to live 72.4 years. In 2014, he could expect to live 76.2 years. The way life expectancy works, however, is that the longer you *do* live, the longer you can expect *to* live. That doesn't stretch out to infinity, of course, but there is a 41 percent chance of the average male living to age 85 and a 20 percent chance of making it to age 90.

Why is this a detour sign? From a retirement income planning perspective, it means that a male who needs $1,000 per month for an extra nine years (age 76 to age 85) will need an extra $108,000 in income. If he lives to be 90, he'll need another $60,000. This does not take inflation into account. If someone needed $60,000 to make ends meet in 1994, that same individual would need approximately $96,000 in 2014 figuring for a modest 3 percent inflation rate. (Source www.usinflationcalculator.com)

# Timing of Returns

As everyone knows, the market does not move in a straight line. It has more ups and downs than a fiddler's elbow at a square dance. The bulls stampede for a while and then the bears take over when the market recedes. All that is normal behavior for the stock market, although I must say that since the turn of the 21$^{st}$ century the market has behaved more erratically than usual. This matters most when you are on the threshold of retirement, and you have to pull money out of a market-based account in order to pay your bills. People may talk about average returns of the market and how, in the end, it all works out to be a net gain, but this does not necessarily hold true for an individual who retires right as the market takes a severe, prolonged drop. It is called the "Sequence-of-Returns" trap, and it can spell trouble for a retiree wishing to enjoy the "golden years" without the fear of running out of resources.

The traditional strategy proposed by financial advisors who are stockbrokers instead of independent fiduciaries has been to "hold on" during these down times and let the averages take care of you. Anyone who has fallen victim to the

"Sequence-of-Returns" trap can readily testify as to the fallacy of such a philosophy.

With a solely market-based retirement strategy, losses during the first few years of one's retirement can have greater negative impact than losses in one's later years. Take two identical retirement portfolios, each valued at, let's say, $250,000 each. Give each an annual rate of return of 6.6 percent. Now assign each an annual drawdown of $12,500, plus 3 percent per year for inflation. Leave everything the same in these two portfolios — same annual returns, positive or negative — except change the order, or the sequence, in which the gains and losses occurred. Remember, these are stock market-based **retirement** portfolios intended to provide an annual salary, or income, for the owners. Let's call them Investor A and Investor B.

Investor A takes some sizable losses during the first three years of retirement when the market records three consecutive years of losses (this actually happened from 2000 to 2003) to the tune of -11.2 percent, -18.5 percent, and -2.9 percent. While this was going on, Investor A was withdrawing $12,500 per year, and each year added 3 percent to accommodate for inflation ($12,875 in Year 2, $13,261.25 in Year 3 and so on). Once Investor A gets past the first three years, he enjoys 13 years without a single negative return on his investments. In fact, one year his portfolio grew by over 19 percent! However, 16 years into his retirement his portfolio has shrunk to $44,624. Two years later, at the age of 79, he runs out of money.

Investor B has **the same returns** of the market that Investor A has, only at different times. During his first three years of retirement, he enjoys positive returns of 15.8 percent, 22.1 percent, and 12.6 percent. Year 4 sees a -3.5 percent return. Over the next 13 years, his portfolio twice generates negative returns. Sixteen years into Investor B's retirement, his portfolio grows to $540,983. At the end of 30 years, Investor B still has money in his account.

The hardest part for us to wrap our head around is that it is possible that Investor A and Investor B both experience an average annual rate of return of 6.6 percent and have such radically different outcomes. As the example illustrated, we can have the same gains and losses in identical portfolios, but the order in which those gains and losses occur **in retirement** can produce vastly different outcomes.

It may seem counterintuitive, but there is no direct correlation between the **average** rate of return and the **actual** income that will end up in your pocket during your retirement years. The moral of the story is this: If you leave 100 percent of your nest egg exposed to the volatility of the market and the sequence of returns, you may not have the lifetime income for which you were hoping.

So what is a near-retiree to do? As the Forbes magazine article cited earlier in this book, "This is why it may make sense, shortly before you retire, to put a portion of your savings in a **fixed annuity** that will provide a guaranteed income stream for a set period of time, usually until death. Doing so will help guard against potential market downturns." This is of course just one way to cope with your need for income in retirement, but it is one worth discussing with your financial professional.

(Source: Forbes, June 10, 2013 "How Much to Withdraw from Retirement Savings," Larry Rosenthal)

---

# Distribution

A fixed-rate annuity is not a drawdown vehicle. Annuities rely on distribution. In some ways, distribution is almost the opposite of drawdown. When you purchase a lump-sum traditional fixed annuity, you know upfront that your principal is guaranteed, your interest rate is guaranteed, and you know exactly how much income you will be receiving every month for the rest of your life, even if you live to be 107. **Distribution** is based on actuarial tables that take into account your life expectancy, the cash value of your annuity and the age at which you begin your payouts. It doesn't matter if the market goes up, down or sideways — when you purchase an annuity and opt for lifetime distribution, you can count on receiving the same check for the rest of your life. From what my clients tell me, that may not be as significant when you are 45 or 50 as it is when you reach age 70 or 80.

I'm not going to explain the nuts and bolts of annuities here because that is the focus of our entire next chapter. However, here is a quick comparison between drawdown of a typical investment and distribution from an annuity.

| Investment drawdown | Annuity* distribution |
| --- | --- |
| Investment is subject to market fluctuations | Annuity value is guaranteed (principal and interest) |
| Payments come from cashing in investments | Payments are predetermined by actuarial tables |
| You may outlive your money | Income can be guaranteed for your lifetime |

*Annuity guarantees are provided by the claims-paying ability of the issuing insurer.

# CHAPTER 10

# The Misunderstood Annuity

Have you ever heard unflattering hearsay about an individual and formed a negative opinion, only to later meet the person face-to-face and develop a genuine friendship? I hate to admit it, but I've done that more than once in my lifetime. It seems to be human nature to do so — to believe opinions instead of gathering facts. This is especially true if the opinions are those of close friends or people you trust.

Sometimes negative remarks about people are nothing more sinister than idle gossip — a repetition of something we have heard. At other times, however, an ulterior motive may be lurking in the shadows.

The annuity is a financial instrument that in my opinion has been the victim of some unfair and untrue publicity in recent years. Whether I'm doing one of my financial seminars or researching the internet, I come across a great deal of misinformation about annuities. Some of it is so blatantly untrue and void of foundation that it makes me wonder if there is a malicious propaganda mill somewhere responsible for starting the rumors. Sometimes there is an element of truth in what the article says — but you don't always get the whole story.

Preconceived notions about annuities are sometimes deeply rooted in those who depend on what they hear and do not research the facts. It sometimes reminds me of superstitions, old wives tales, conspiracy theories and urban legends. People swear by such things that have no basis in fact. Sometimes folks come to my seminars with these prejudices based on how annuities functioned

100 years ago, not the new types of annuities, which function so differently I sometimes wish they were called something else.

Before I address some of the hearsay, rumors and "old news" about annuities, note what some high-profile commentators have said about them recently:

- "By covering at least their basic expenses with lifetime income annuities, retirees are able to focus on discretionary funds as a source for enjoyment." ~ **Wharton School of Financial Institutions Center,** Professor David R. Babbel and Professor Craig B. Merrill, "Investing your Lump Sum at Retirement"
- "If you do not want to take any risks but still want to play the stock market, a good index annuity might be right for you." ~ "The Road to Wealth Revised" by **Suze Orman**
- **The American public.** Voting with their pocketbooks, Americans purchased a record $54.5 billion in **fixed index annuities** in 2015, according to a report by LIMRA, a worldwide insurance research organization.

---

# Evolution of Annuities

In ancient Rome, citizens entered into contracts whereby they would receive annual payments, or stipends, called *annua* in Latin. The contracts could guarantee the payments for a number of years or until death. This was commonplace among soldiers who feared their families would be left without material support should they be killed in battle. Soldiers would pool their money, thus forming the first fraternal insurance association. When the proceeds were paid out in annual stipends according to a contract (instead of a lump sum), the first annuities were born. This was long before actuaries ground a finer point on such contractual agreements. That wouldn't happen until the industrial revolution came to Europe in the 17th century.

Annuities made their way to America in 1759 when they were used to provide lifetime income for retired church pastors in Pennsylvania. Then, in 1812, a life insurance company began offering annuities to the public. Nonetheless, interest in annuities lagged until the stock market crash in 1929. Annuities came into their own when people became disillusioned with banks and the stock market. When insurance companies began offering guaranteed principal, guaranteed interest and a guaranteed lifetime income, it made a lot of sense to consumers. People were willing to exchange a lower rate of return for the guarantees. Also, consumers understood that even though they were guaranteed a lifetime income, if their lives ended prematurely, the insurance company kept the balance of their funds. If the annuitant collected only two payments and then died, the insurance company had fulfilled its obligation, and the annuitant's heirs received nothing while the insurance company prospered. By the same token, if the annuitant lived well past his life expectancy, he prospered while the insurance company continued payments. It was seen as a fair trade off. These traditional annuities still exist today but are not as popular as they once were.

By 1952, low annuity interest rates had become less attractive to consumers who preferred the growth potential of the stock market. They did, however, enjoy the tax-deferred status of the annuity, so insurance companies designed the **variable** annuity, which offers tax deferral but also invests in the stock market. In simple terms, variable annuities offered participation in the market with no guarantees to principal or interest. But if the market performed well, the gains produced would be tax-deferred. Variable annuities, like equities, worked well in a bull market but lost value when markets corrected.

The introduction of variable annuities muddied the waters somewhat when it came to public opinion. Prior to variable annuities, people had always associated the word "annuity" with guaranteed principal and interest. Now, consumers could lose money in an annuity. You can imagine the coffee-cup conversations taking place during a market down cycle. When people complained about losing money in their "annuity," unless they specified that it was a *variable* annuity that was the culprit, its distant cousin, the *fixed* annuity, would incur equal blame, which is when the false information began to spread.

Also, with variable annuities came an inheritance feature offered as an option for which there was a fee. The life insurance tack-on is often mistaken as a principal guarantee — it is if you don't mind dying to claim it. While you are living, if your variable annuity loses its value, that value is as lost as if it were the value of shares in a mutual fund that lost money.

Variable annuities are still popular with stockbrokers, and many investors enjoy the tax-deferred aspects of them. You can sock lots of dollars into the stock market and defer paying taxes on gains until you withdraw them. While that may be an advantage of taxable investments, I still recommend you seek a second opinion. The contract you currently own may be less effective in meeting your goals than new annuity contracts available today. The IRS has a provision for you to "trade in" a current contract for a newer model without incurring taxes. We will go over details after we have completed this overview.

## Fixed Index Annuities

A revolution of sorts came on the scene when baby boomers began retiring. Boomer investors wanted the upside potential of the stock market without the risk of loss of principal. Boomers liked the idea of a guaranteed lifetime income but were not too keen on the idea of annuitization — a term meaning to convert the balance of the annuity into an income stream. With the old-style traditional fixed annuities, annuitization meant that if you received just one or two payments from your income stream and then died, your heirs got nothing, and the insurance company kept the balance.

Insurance companies, like any other for-profit enterprise, sensed this new mood of consumers and retooled. They put their actuaries and product design people to work and came out with a new product that would still guarantee the principal but allow the growth of a stock market index, such as the S&P 500, to serve as the basis for calculating interest credits. In other words, instead of a stated interest rate like traditional fixed annuities, these new annuities would gain ground when the market rose but would not lose ground when the market fell. They dubbed the product the "fixed index annuity." It was fixed, as opposed to variable with a guarantee of principal, and followed an index to calculate interest credits. As a trade-off for guaranteed principal, consumers accept a cap on gains. In other words, if the index gained 15 points in a year, the annuity would grow accordingly *up to a cap.* Caps vary from one insurance carrier to another and are subject to change. One popular contract I am aware of has a cap of 8 percent. If the market soars one year and goes up 20 percent, the annuity grows by 8 percent. If the market crashes the next year, the annuity has zero growth, but the value from the year before is locked in and cannot be lost due to market volatility. This is often called the "ratchet-reset" feature.

---

## Income Riders

In the mid-2000s, **income riders** were introduced as an option to fixed index annuities. This made a guaranteed lifetime income available without having to annuitize. This rider adds a separate "ledger" account to the annuity that is used for the purposes of calculating the lifetime income, which is why it is referred to as an "income account," as opposed to the actual balance of the annuity, which is referred to as the "base account." The income account grows at a specific annual compound rate of interest — usually 5-8 percent — until the annuitant decides to "turn on" the income stream. Meanwhile, should the annuitant die, the value of the annuity can be passed on to heirs.

This new development seemed to scratch retiring baby boomers where they itched. The figure mentioned earlier of 39.3 billion (total of fixed index annuities sold in 2013) was up 16 percent from the previous year. This phenomenon was spurred on by the availability of the relatively new GLIR (guaranteed lifetime income rider) or GLWB (guaranteed lifetime withdrawal benefit). The "itch" was the nagging worry among many boomers that they could, now that people are living longer, outlive their resources, lose their independence and end up becoming a burden on those they love. Many financial advisors who specialize in retirement income planning were delighted to be able to offer these products. For many retiring consumers, the fact that their principal was guaranteed and their income could last throughout their lives served to end the hand-wringing and sleepless nights of worrying what the vagaries of the stock market might do to their portfolios.

As if to put sprinkles on top of the sundae, insurance companies offered another solution to a nagging worry over long-term care when they introduced long-term care riders to fixed index annuities. These provisions made it possible for those who found the terms of traditional long-term care insurance policies untenable or the premiums too expensive to have an alternative strategy. There are way too many variations in these long-term care riders to examine each one here. Each insurance company is packaging the LTC rider a little differently. The bottom line is that some who could not qualify for LTC insurance for health reasons and others who waited too long and found it too expensive to purchase may have a welcome option available to them that was not there before.

## Finding the Right Fit

Today there are as many types of annuities as there are models of automobiles. So when you hear someone talking about an annuity, you have to qualify it by asking what type of annuity the person is referring to. I have found that even folks who own annuities don't often know what type they have. It's not because annuities are overly complicated; it's because they don't know what questions to ask. Just like the options on automobiles can customize a car to your needs, annuities can be tailored to fit your specific retirement needs.

## Annuities Still Evolving

Annuities are still evolving. While I was writing this book, a far-reaching tax ruling was finalized on July 1, 2014, when the U.S. Department of Treasury and the Internal Revenue Service amended the required minimum distribution (RDM) regulations for certain deferred annuities. In the past, annuities funded by IRAs or 401(k)s were required to begin distributions by age 70 ½. Today, retirees may live to be 85 or 95 years old. To plan for this, retirees can now use a combination strategy that allows for part of their savings to purchase guaranteed income for life and a smaller portion (up to 25 percent or $125,000, whichever is less) to be invested in a qualified longevity annuity contract (QLAC). Under the new ruling, the QLAC can continue to grow tax deferred until the retirees become 80 years or older. There are also a few bells and whistles that go along with this ruling, not to mention some limitations like a lack of liquidity that makes the QLACs virtually irrevocable. We'll go over the details when we get to the QLAC subheading, but I want you to know that this is a powerful step forward in ensuring that you don't outlive your income.

# Fiduciaries

Aside from what I call "accidental misinformation," there are some financial professionals who intentionally cast annuities in a bad light because they can't offer them. Financial advisors who are stockbrokers only and who aren't license to sell insurance will not have annuities in their "tool box" of financial strategies and solutions. Typically, they are limited to what their mother company gives them in the way of products. Wall Streeters have historically steered their clients away from annuities. Naturally, if they can't offer a product, they cannot benefit financially from it. Is it likely that a Ford dealer would recommend that you buy a Buick? I doubt it, unless, of course, he also sold Buicks.

Advisors who are not licensed in insurance are not allowed to give advice on subjects or products for which they have not been trained. By the same token, insurance agents who are not licensed to sell securities are not allowed to offer advice on equities. To get fair and balanced advice, you need to seek out an independent advisor who has access to both and can fit the problem/solution puzzle pieces together correctly. Insurance agents are required to be licensed for each state in which they conduct business and must be appointed by each insurance carrier they represent.

A **fiduciary** advisor is legally and ethically required by law to advise clients according to what is in their best interests. Fiduciary is a legal designation which, in the financial advisory community, sets a high standard. Fiduciaries must advise their clients and prospective clients according to whatever is in the client's best interest, irrespective of the advisor's own personal profit. Fiduciaries should present the pros and cons of any option and let the client decide on his or her own. Since our firm is a fiduciary firm, we have brought all of the advisors and insurance professionals under one roof and have expanded our tools to offer both securities and insurance products.

# What Others Are Saying

What about the media? If you research current media sources over the past five years, you'll find a mountain of positive messages about annuities that is hard to miss. It is a real eye-opener for those who haven't taken a fresh look at annuities in 10 years or more.

For instance, did you catch this one? In 2010, Jane Bryant Quinn, the revered financial columnist for The Washington Post with a prior reputation for holding a hard and fast stance against annuities, wrote the surprising article, "Set Up a Future Income With a New-Style Annuity." She said, "Praise for these contracts is surprising, coming from me... But for people without pensions, the guarantees themselves are attractive, despite the fees. In fact, they're more generous than they should be..."

What changed the columnist's mind? Annuities had changed, and she caught it.

I have noticed this trend: When articles in financial magazines slam annuities, you can just follow the money trail to see why. Scan through the magazine and see who the advertisers are and that investing philosophy they share. You will likely find that the magazine is chocked full of advertisements from brokerage houses and Wall Street types. A negative portrayal of annuities advances their cause.

Many people are receiving annuity payments and do not realize it. For example, the TIAA in TIAA-CREF stands for "Teachers Insurance and Annuity Association." Many pension plans are structured with annuities at the core. TSPs (Thrift Savings Plans) for retired federal employees or the uniformed services are annuities. Teachers' retirement funds are annuities.

## Single Premium Immediate Annuity (SPIA)

Retirees who want to begin receiving payments immediately often purchase a single premium immediate annuity (SPIA). As the name implies, in return for your one lump-sum premium, the insurance company promises to make payments to you for the rest of your life, or for the term you specify. Usually, people who purchase a SPIA opt for the guaranteed lifetime payout.

The amount of your distribution will depend on your age, gender and designated payout.

**Here are some examples**:

Mr. Smith, age 60, deposits $100,000 into a SPIA and opts to receive monthly checks beginning in 30 days. If he chooses the **"single life only,"** he will receive the highest payment because the insurance company is accepting the lowest risk. This means that he will receive guaranteed payments for his entire lifetime, but no money will be passed on to beneficiaries. At current rates as of 2014, Mr. Smith could expect to receive $512 per month. However, Mr. Smith might want to insure that someone collects at least 10 years of payments. After all, he may meet his demise only three months into his retirement. No problem. The insurance company has already thought of that option. Mr. Smith can choose the **"single life with 10 years"** and his named beneficiaries are guaranteed to receive a monthly check if he is not here to receive it himself during those first 10 years. Surprisingly, this option only reduces Mr. Smith's monthly check by $21, to $491. Mr. Smith can even opt for **"single life for 20 years."** In this case, Mr. Smith would receive $448 per month for his lifetime and if he died within the first 20 years, his beneficiary would receive his check for the remainder of the 20 years. What if Mr. Smith wants to make sure either he or his beneficiaries receive 100 percent of his original lump sum? That option is called **"single life with installment refund."** In this case, Mr. Smith's monthly distribution would be $478 for his lifetime. If he dies before receiving payments equal to his original lump sum premium, then his beneficiaries would receive installments until the remaining premium was paid out. There is even an option for someone who does not want a guaranteed lifetime payment. If Mr. Smith wants his distribution over a set number of years, he can choose either the **"10-year period certain"** or the **"20-year period certain."** In either case, his SPIA will pay him or, if need be, his beneficiaries the stated payments for the chosen term. If Mr. Smith chose the 10-year term, the distributions will be $866 per month. If he doubles the term to 20 years, the payments will be $531 per month. Finally, Mr. Smith might have in mind to provide for his wife, who is also age 60. In this case, he would choose the **"joint life only"** option. Now, this couple will receive guaranteed lifetime payments of $444 as long as *either* of them is alive. At this point, something interesting happens in the annuitization calculations. Mr. Smith could opt for the **"joint life with 10 years certain"** or the **"joint life with 20 years certain"** or the **"joint life with in-**

**stallment refund"** (explained above) and each of these options would reduce his monthly lifetime payment by less than $5 a month. In essence, for less $5 a month, Mr. Smith and his wife could look their heirs in the eyes and assure them that someone (the annuitants or the heirs) will receive benefits from the SPIA for the time designated.

This factual scenario demonstrates the many choices available within a single type of annuity — in this case, the SPIA. So it's not fair to blame the insurance carrier if John Doe purchased a $100,000 SPIA and died of a heart attack three months later and the heirs received zero. Who is to blame? Maybe no one? It's possible that Mr. Doe purchased this contract with the sole intention of funding his lifetime retirement, and he was willing to exchange any inheritance options for the highest possible paycheck. After all, not everyone wants to leave a legacy. Some people want to spend all of their resources while they are alive and not leave anything to heirs. It's a free country, and that's OK. I once heard a man say that it was his wish to write his final check to cover his funeral expenses and have that check bounce for insufficient funds! I also saw a bumper sticker on a very expensive motor home which read: "We are spending our children's inheritance."

However, it's also possible that Mr. Doe was not aware of all of his options. In fact, it's a rare day when someone comes into my office or attends one of my seminars who can list even three of these 10 distribution options. This underscores the value of working with a knowledgeable retirement planner who can clearly explain your options and the features and benefits of each.

In general, people purchase SPIAs for the following reasons:

- **Guaranteed Income:** Knowing you cannot outlive your savings addresses the No. 1 fear of retirees. The annuity provides guaranteed income for life or for the years you specify.
- **Easy:** Immediate pay annuities are "get it and forget it" contracts that release you from the need to watch the market, track interest rates or monitor dividends. Once you sign the contract, the amount of your income payments will always stay the same.
- **Guaranteed Principal:** Your principal is guaranteed by the assets of the insurance company holding your annuity contract and is not subject to fluctuations in the stock or bond market. Insurance companies

have an excellent reputation and a long history of honoring their contracts.

- **Competitive Interest:** Interest rates used to calculate your distributions are generally higher than the prevailing CD or Treasury rates. Also, since part of your payment is a return of principal, your payments are higher than if you were receiving interest only.

Retirees often fund their SPIA using the proceeds from the sale of their home or business, matured CDs, the sale of investments or the settlement of a life insurance policy. Because the lump sum premium is not being paid from tax-deferred money, a portion of each payment will be excluded from income tax as a return of principal. The contract will specify the excluded amount for each year. However, SPIAs can also be funded by IRAs, SEPs, lump sum distributions from qualified retirement plans, and other "qualified" money that has been exempt by the IRS from income taxes. The resulting **Qualified Immediate Annuity** will produce a monthly check that is wholly subject to income taxes, because taxes were paid on these funds. Also, as with all annuities, distributions before you're age 59 ½ may be subject to an additional 10 percent federal penalty for early withdrawals.

## Fixed Annuity

A fixed annuity is traditionally purchased to accumulate assets for retirement. Your money grows tax-deferred, which means you earn interest not only on your principal but also on any previously credited interest. Annuities have a penalty for early withdrawal, called a "surrender charge," but this penalty disappears after a specified period, typically between three and 10 years.

To demonstrate the power of compounding interest that occurs in these annuities, if you pay a $100,000 premium into an annuity with 3.35 percent interest, three years from now you will have $110,390.43. If you opt for five years, it will grow to $117,910.48. If you choose 10 years, your nest egg will reach $139,028.81. Remember, you are using Uncle Sam's money (money you would normally pay in taxes) to grow your nest egg in this deferred annuity. When you are ready to retire, you have several income options, such as the guaranteed lifetime income or the many other choices we identified in the previous section. You will also pay income taxes on the distributions, but you may be in a lower tax bracket.

Some people scoff at the idea of regularly putting retirement savings into a tax-deferred, fixed-rate annuity. Like so many people, these scoffers have been conditioned to believe that it is always better to invest in the stock market if you have at least 10 years for the money to grow. That is what businessman Peter Heimdahl thought until he did the math. In an article published in Business Record, Sept. 17, 2006, Heimdahl said he had been investing money in stock and bond funds in his 401(k) for 30 years. When he looked at the end result, he was dismayed. In the article titled, "Why I Love My Fixed Annuity," he wrote, "Given how much money I lost in my 401(k) stock funds (they still haven't recovered from the 2000 crash), had I placed all my savings in a fixed annuity averaging a 5 percent return instead of in stocks, I would be almost $200,000 ahead."

MassMutual Financial Group released a study in 2008 showing that for the years between 1965 and 2006, "Incorporating **a fixed income annuity** in a retirement income account yielded greater long term wealth for an investor— along with more income security — than a portfolio of equity and bond investments alone, even in an 'up' market." The study tested four strategies for investing retirement income and found that incremental purchases of fixed annuities — called **annuity laddering** — produced more liquidity and more guaranteed lifetime income. While past performance isn't a guarantee of future results, this study did not include the market crash of 2008, which would have further affected the stock and bond scenarios, but would have left the guaranteed fixed annuities completely unscathed.

Annuities may not be suitable for everyone, and without seeing your particular circumstances I can't comment on whether they have a place in your portfolio, but I will say it is always worth looking into new things and increasing our financial literacy and knowledge base. Wouldn't you agree?

# Growth Potential With Guarantees

The younger generation of consumers who desired the guarantees of a fixed annuity combined with the upside potential of the stock market wanted to have their cake and eat it too. In large measure, the FIA delivers on both counts. With the fixed index annuity, you have a guaranteed minimum interest rate (floor), plus the potential to earn interest credits based on a stock market index such as the S&P 500. In exchange for the guarantees, the carrier limits your upside potential with a cap.

Initially, fixed-rate annuities received mixed reviews. In fact, in the first year, consumers committed less than a half billion dollars to this new breed of annuity. By 2009, however, following the 2008-2009 market crash, consumers decided that "capped" potential coupled with guaranteed principal may be a good way to go. Sales shot up to $30 billion. Since then, retirees have been increasingly purchasing fixed index annuities.

Many insurance companies are now offering a bonus to attract consumers. As of the writing of this book, bonuses range from 5 to 10 percent and come packaged in various ways depending on the carrier. Typically, if the carrier offers a bonus of, say, 10 percent, when you pay a $100,000 premium, you will receive an additional $10,000. However, this bonus amount is usually not available to you until after a vesting period is over, and often is only available under a specified income stream. In many cases, if you surrender the annuity early or don't take the required income stream, you will lose the bonus amount. Also, some annuities that offer a bonus feature involve longer surrender charge periods, lower caps and other limitations

In addition to offering a fixed rate strategy, a fixed index annuity typically credits interest annually based on the performance of an index. The index interest crediting strategies will vary from insurance company to insurance company, but generally calculate interest using one of the following modifiers:

- **Spread:** If the index gain is 10 percent and the spread/asset fee is 2 percent, then the annuity would be credited 8 percent.

- **Participation Rate:** The insurance company sets the participation rate, for instance, at 90 percent. Your annuity will be credited interest equal to 90 percent of the index performance (usually the S&P 500) tied to your annuity.
- **Interest Rate Cap:** Your annuity is credited interest equal to the index increase up to the stated cap.

Bells and whistles vary from company to company, so it is prudent to work with an independent fiduciary who specializes in retirement income planning to help ensure your annuity is tailored to your needs for earnings withdrawals, bonus credits, surrender fees, index links, payout options and more. I cringe at the thought of someone buying a fixed index annuity online — and it does happen — because even though these products are fairly straightforward, it is unwise to make any financial decision this significant without professional guidance.

## Annuities With Riders

These annuities simply combine two elements to facilitate one strategy: a fixed index annuity with an income rider attached. The combination has become so popular that most people who purchase index annuities (three out of four, according to www.fixedannuityfacts.com) elect to include the income rider option. One metaphor that has been used to illustrate how these work is a motorcycle with a side car. You can't purchase a stand-alone income rider. It doesn't work that way. You need the base annuity to go along with it. You can, however, purchase an FIA without the income rider if you wish.

Another illustration I heard recently is that of a hybrid car, which has two engines, one gasoline powered and the other electric, to explain the two accounts that go with annuities that have riders: (a) base account and (b) income account. They each function differently, but both propel the vehicle.

Both accounts start with the same balance. Let's say that your premium was $200,000, and the company gives you a 10 percent bonus. Both accounts are immediately valued at $220,000. The value of the *base account* can earn interest credits tied to the movement of the stock market index, whereas the *income account* — which is a ledger account and not accessible in a lump sum — grows at a rate fixed and declared in the contract, called the "roll up" rate.

When you decide to trigger the income rider so that you can receive payments for life, the payments are based on your age at the time you activated the income. Products vary, but typically the percentage of payout is one point below your age. In other words, if you are age 70 when you activate your income, you will receive 6 percent of the account value for life. If you are age 75, then you will receive 6.5 percent of the account value for life. If you unexpectedly pass away after receiving only 12 months of payments (payments may be taken in monthly increments if desired), the unused balance will go to your beneficiaries as specified by you in the contract. Some contracts have provisions that allow two to three times the value of the annuity to be paid out over a two or three-year period if you require long-term care.

# 1035 Exchange

Once people discover the evolution of annuities in recent years, they may realize that their current annuity is no longer meeting their needs. If you and your retirement planner decide that you need to make a change, the IRS has provisions in place to enable you to avoid triggering a taxable event. One is a 1035 exchange, named after Section 1035 of the Internal Revenue Code, which spells out the details of the provision.

To qualify for a 1035 exchange, you must follow specific guidelines:
- You may not receive a check. The original contract must be **directly exchanged** for a new contract.
- You may not exchange an annuity contract for a life insurance contract.
- You may exchange a life insurance contract for an annuity.

Even though there are no taxes involved in the 1035 Exchange, there may be fees assessed by the insurance company. Also, the surrender charges may have expired on the original contract, while new surrender charges are applied to the new contract. Here again, it is best to review all of the pros and cons with a trusted retirement planner who is fully aware of your financial goals.

---

# Qualified Longevity Annuity Contract (QLAC)

As referred to earlier in this chapter, as of July 1, 2014, the U.S. Department of Treasury and the Internal Revenue Service make it possible for people to fund longevity annuities with monies invested in IRAs and 401(k)s and similar employer-sponsored individual retirement plans.

A longevity annuity is any annuity contract — fixed, fixed index, variable or hybrid — that is intended to continue to accumulate tax-deferred beyond the age of 70 ½. To be designated as a **qualified longevity annuity contract (QLAC)** the contract must state its intention either in the contract or in an insurance certificate, rider or endorsement.

In a nutshell, IRA and 401(k) monies that are used to fund a QLAC are exempt from the required minimum distributions (RMD) that apply to other tax-deferred investments. In this case, retirees can purchase a QLAC with the full intention of letting it grow until the retiree reaches the age of 85. This allows retirees to fully enjoy their retirement incomes until age 85, knowing that if they live to be 85, their QLACs can be triggered into a new income stream.

"All Americans deserve security in their later years and need effective tools to make the most of their hard-earned savings," said J. Mark Iwry, senior advisor to the secretary of the Treasury and deputy assistant secretary for Retirement and Health Policy. The U.S. Treasury department press release continued quoting Iwry as follows: "As boomers approach retirement and life expectancies increase, longevity income annuities can be an important option to help Americans plan for retirement and ensure they have a regular stream of income for as long as they live." Now, these annuities are only appropriate for those who have enough resources to get them through the earlier part of retirement but who may be seeking to have guaranteed income later on in life. QLACs aren't liquid, and the contracts are often irrevocable once in-force, so, while I encourage you to investigate this as an option, I would also caution that you do your homework thoroughly and be sure of your intentions before pulling the trigger.

- Participants can use up to 25 percent of their account balance or $125,000 (whichever is less). Cost-of-living increases aren't guaranteed, but are determined on a yearly as-needed basis.
- The contract allows for a "return of premium" death benefit if the retiree dies before receiving the premiums paid for the annuity — this feature is generally available at an added cost.

## Consult a Professional

One thing is probably clear by now. Annuities and the laws that affect them are constantly evolving. Because so many options are available, it is prudent to consult a fiduciary retirement planner to decide if an annuity has a place in your retirement portfolio.

# CHAPTER 11

# The Round Table Retirement Process to S.H.I.E.L.D. Your Future

T he shield has been around since the dawn of man. Our ancient ancestors used shields to defend themselves from the rocks, arrows or blades of their enemies. When times got tough, they sometimes turned their hand-held defensive armor into offensive weapons to clobber their opponents. These shields often weighed 15 to 35 pounds, so they could do plenty

of damage. But it was Alexander the Great who changed the course of history by use of the shield. Even though he was only 20 years old when he inherited the throne of Macedonia, Alexander had grand ideas. He planned to conquer to world. By ingeniously using the shield, Alexander created a virtually impenetrable wall of warriors.

Here's how he did it. The shields, called hoplons, were bowl-shaped discs allowing them to be supported on the shoulder. Also, new grips and straps improved mobility of these 3-foot diameter shields. Instead of each man protecting his own body, warriors advanced in tight formation with each soldier using the left part of his shield to protect the right side of the soldier to his left. At the same time, these soldiers used their free hand to expertly stab the enemy with spears that were 7 to 9 feet long. The result was an armed shield wall, called a phalanx, which plowed down enemy forces.

As gruesome as this may sound, this is war and this is history. With this technique, Alexander the Great was able to beat the odds. One of his most famous conquests occurred when his army of 47,000 defeated the Persian army of 1 million near Gaugamela. Unfortunately, Alexander the Great died from malarial fever at age 32 but he never saw defeat and met his goal to become conqueror of the then-known world.

Financial success is also dependent on choosing the right shield for the job. In ancient times, there were shields made of wood, bronze and even leather. It was the design of the shield that was the defining difference. Our retirement is under attack from such enemies as inflation, taxation, longevity and probate costs. There are plenty of shields out there, but we want the optimal shield — the one that may help protect our retirement as time marches on.

We developed this process after years of experience and have found it to be the most efficient way to uncover and build the picture that makes up your puzzle that is your retirement. Our process is trademarked and we feel makes for a great experience. We must get to know you and see if we have a common ground from which to build a relationship. You must have realistic expectations, and we must be able to bring value to you. A round table allows everyone to sit at the head and everyone brings value so we prefer an environment of discussion and frankness. The issues we address when working with you are yours, not ours, so we want to make sure you are 100 percent on board with our thought processes. I have outlined it below. Even though there are four steps, the process may take more or less than four meetings because everyone is unique, and we work toward your comfort.

1. **Evaluation Visit**
   - Get to know one another, and determine if we are a good fit to work together
2. **Strategy Visit**
   - Review your situation and determine what strategies should be considered

3. **Implementation Visit**

- Recommendations are presented and, if agreed upon, are executed

4. **Presentation Visit**

- Final presentation of the overall plan, delivery of any pertinent documentation

To the right is the shield that we use at Retirement Solutions Group, Inc. You'll see that it has four interlocking mini-shields — insurance, investments, legacy and estate. The estate piece appropriately rounds out our protection since we don't want to make it to and through retirement only to have Uncle Sam or someone else claim what rightly belongs to our heirs. Imagine if your estate was worth $500,000 and it was all in a

qualified IRA so you had not paid taxes yet. Also for this illustration, imagine you have two beneficiaries. The IRA is taxed within nine months of your passing if not properly structured and Uncle Sam would get approximately half, or $250,000. Each beneficiary would receive 25 percent, or $125,000, making Uncle Sam your biggest beneficiary. Most of this chapter will focus on estate planning, but first, let's quickly address the other three aspects of our shield.

# Insurance

Insurance, especially when it comes to health care, can shore up the unknowns in our retirement budget. In Chapter 5, we went into great detail examining Medicare, Medigap insurance, long-term care insurance and Medicaid. If you skimmed over this portion of the book, now might be a good time to revisit that information if you feel your retirement plan leaves you unprotected in this area. Of course, there is no need to go it alone. See an insurance professional but make sure he or she has plenty of experience in this area.

Additionally, in the last chapter, we went over annuities with a fine tooth comb. Annuities are issued by insurance companies, so they belong under this subheading. Usually, our goal with annuities is to create a guaranteed lifetime **income**. We want to know we will not outlive our incomes.

However, one type of insurance is often prematurely discarded at retirement. I'm talking about life insurance. Most of us need to change our thinking. As we would any other asset, include this valuable protection as part of your estate; the government does. Sometimes new retirees are so excited to get rid of the binding business suits, over-scheduled calendars and tiresome commutes which accompany corporate life that they automatically toss out their life insurance policy. Usually, they will reason something like this: "I don't have any minor children depending on me, and my spouse is already taken care of." What they forget is that life insurance serves at least two other major purposes. First, if you've been a successful business owner and/or have a sizeable estate, life insurance can provide ready funds to pay the hefty estate **taxes**. Second, many people want to leave a **legacy** for children, grandchildren, their alma maters or favorite charities. Many couples today have age differences of several years, and women statistically outlive most males. When we said "I do!" and we promised to love, honor and cherish till death do us part, it doesn't have to end then. Life insurance provides a quick and smooth transfer of wealth, and the death benefits are income tax free to the beneficiary. It can bridge the income for your surviving spouse. With many plans today, you can take care of long-term care needs as well.

# Products

In Chapter 6, we took a hard look at Red, Yellow and Green Money. Remember, Red Money is risk money. Red Money products include stocks, bonds, mutual funds, ETFs, REITs, precious metals and other commodities. Green Money is guaranteed money. Yellow Money is for income production where yield or the return of our money is most important. Green Money includes saving accounts, money markets, CDs and fixed annuities. The key, of course, is to move our assets from Red Money to Yellow Money as we approach retirement. We can still have some Red Money products go to diversity and to hedge against inflation, but our first priority is to fortify the Yellow Money to create a guaranteed lifetime income that we cannot outlive.

# Legacy

Some people think that you only leave a legacy by leaving money to your heirs or favorite charity, but everyone leaves a legacy. A legacy is simply what you leave behind — your imprint on your family, your friends and maybe even the world. A friend of mine didn't receive a dime from his grandmother. She simply didn't have it. Nevertheless, she left a legacy — in example and in a letter — of honesty, hard work, integrity and affection. That was worth more to him than a pile of gold. It helped him to remember where he came from and where he was taking the next generation. Other people, who can leave a monetary inheritance, simply choose not to. Their legacy is: "Live it up. Spend it all. Your life is YOUR gift." It's not that these people are selfish; they simply have a strongly held belief and they live their belief. It's OK, and it works for them. However, I find that most of us want to leave both beliefs and money behind for our children, grandchildren and the causes that are close to our hearts. To accomplish this most effectively, most people use the tools of insurance and estate planning. Many years ago, I partnered with an estate planning attorney for this reason.

# Estate Planning

Simply put, estate planning is an ongoing process to ensure that your assets will be managed appropriately in the event that you are incapacitated, and to assure that your estate is distributed/settled (including taxes, which can be 40 percent or higher) in line with your wishes upon your death. Most people work with an attorney experienced in estate law when setting up their estate plan. I do encourage you to have your plan reviewed if purchased prior to 2006 when HIPPA and stretch provisions were added.

Why is it an ongoing process? Things change. We sell a house, buy a new car or welcome a new grandchild. Each of these events can signal a change in our estate plans. Before we tackle the five tools for effective estate planning, I want to share with you a common mistake that too many people make. This scenario shows you just how important it is to know the consequences of each estate planning decision. It also highlights the need to work with a knowledgeable professional.

# Joint Ownership and Probate

Probate is the legal process by which your assets are transferred to your heirs after your death. The process is supervised by the courts and can be a time-consuming and expensive ordeal that is, by law, open to the public. Estate planning is one way to eliminate some of the costs, expense and public scrutiny that is associated with the probate process.

There are many mistaken impressions concerning probate. Consider the case of a retired woman we will call Mary. Mary decides to simply name her three adult sons as joint owners of all her investments, assets and her home. This seems fair and equitable, she reasons — and why not? She had always planned to leave the property to them anyway when she passed away.

But let's play a little "what if." What if Mary's oldest son, whom we will call Scott, now a joint owner of Mary's savings account, gets divorced? That's a pretty common occurrence in today's world, after all. As the law now stands in most states, Mary's ex-daughter-in-law will end up with a sizable portion of her money. Is that what Mary intended? Potentially not…

What if Mary's second son, Devon, who becomes joint owner of her home, is in an unfortunate automobile accident? He is unhurt, but a lawsuit ensues, and Devon is found at fault in the accident. The judgment is greater than the limits of his car insurance policy. The home is listed as one of Devon's assets in the lawsuit, and strangers end up owning Mary's home. Ouch!

What if Mary's third son, Mark, falls on tough times and has to file for bankruptcy? Mark is a joint owner of Mary's brokerage accounts. Creditors negotiate for the settlement of unpaid obligations, and the accounts are taken. The same thing would happen if Mark was to become incapacitated, couldn't work, couldn't pay his bills and creditors took legal action.

What if Mary decides that she wants to buy a second home in Florida? She may have the assets, but she no longer has the freedom. She will now have to get the approval and signatures of all the joint owners of her assets before she can do what she wishes with the funds required to buy the property.

Finally, what if Mary decided to keep things simple by naming only her oldest son Mark, as joint owner of all her property and investments? Additionally, what if Mary asked him to divide her property equally with his brothers at the time of her death and he did not experience any of the setbacks listed above? Unfortunately, because there is a not a legally binding document, Mark can keep all of the money or distribute it as he sees fit. Even if Mary stated her wishes in her will, joint ownership causes the title to pass to the designated joint owner, and may not pass through the will. So Mary's wishes — to transfer her remaining assets to her heirs as quickly and easily as possible — may backfire. Instead of being a source of joy, her legacy could create lasting family conflict. I know this isn't a concern for you because families never have disagreements or argue, especially about money. I say this in jest, of course.

Business owners often find themselves in business with spouses and family members of deceased partners because of poor estate planning.

**There are two types of non-spousal joint ownership:**

- **Tenants in common:** When two people own property as tenants in common, each of them owns a separate 50 percent. Upon the death of one owner, the other 50 percent does NOT pass to the remaining tenant in common; it may end up in probate. Any transaction needs the approval from both tenants in common.

- **Joint tenants with rights of survivorship (JTWROS):** When two people own property as JTWROS, then upon the death of one owner, the property will pass directly to the remaining owner. In JTWROS, either owner can make a transaction without the consent of the other owner.

## A Better Way

There is a better way for Mary to accomplish her objectives. Surprisingly, most people are not as aware of these two options as a way to avoid probate. Also, all the sad scenarios that we examined in the "what if" game do not apply to the options below because the beneficiaries do not legally own any percentage of your assets while you are living.

- **Transfer on death (TOD) registration:** Check to see if your market investments, mutual funds, cars and real estate can have the TOD provision. It varies from state to state. If so, you can name a beneficiary to the account and, upon your death, it will transfer immediately to the named beneficiary and avoid probate.
- **Payable on death (POD) registration:** Set up your checking, savings and security deposits at banks and credit unions as POD accounts. Name a beneficiary to the account and, upon your death, it will transfer immediately to the named beneficiary and avoid probate.

## Powers of Attorney

Legally designating a power of attorney is important for adults of any age, but it is an imperative first step in estate planning. In the event that you have an accident or illness, and you are unable to communicate your wishes, your power of attorney will act on your behalf. It is best to clarify your wishes in advance in this regard.

**Power of attorney**: a legal document in which you grant someone the authority to act as your representative and to make legal and financial decisions for you. You decide whom you appoint, when the power of attorney takes effect and when it is terminated.

## Health Care Directive

Similar to a power of attorney, this legal document identifies whom you appoint to make health care decisions if you are unable to communicate your wishes. The health care directive limits your named representative to medical and health care issues. This, too, is an important aspect of estate planning.

**There are two ways that health care directives are typically chosen:**

- Designate a health care representative and fill out the necessary document. Be sure you and your designated representative each have a copy of your document. Some people have their doctor retain a copy in the medical files. Generally, you will choose a spouse, close relative or close friend to represent you.
- Write a living will to specify your medical wishes. This will include treatments that you may or may not agree with or whether or not you want life-sustaining medical intervention if you are in a coma or terminally ill. Be sure to review this document with family and friends so that your decisions are honored.

## Beneficiary Deeds

A third estate-planning tool is a beneficiary deed. This is a legal document that states who will receive your property and real estate at the time of your death. It's quick, it's easy and it avoids probate. If this sounds familiar, you're right. We went over the two types of beneficiary deeds at the end of the section on joint ownership. For some property, you will want to use a transfer on death (TOD) registration and for other property it would be appropriate to use a payable on death (POD) registration. I wanted to revisit this because beneficiary deeds are so important. Each state differs, so it is best to consult with the attorney who is part of your retirement planning team. Remember, with a beneficiary deed, the owner holds all rights to the property. You can sell the property, rent it, refinance it, remodel it or do anything you like without the consent of the beneficiary.

# Letter of Instruction

A personal letter to your loved ones intended to be read after you are gone may just be the most important and beloved letter you will ever compose. No, it is not designed to take the place of your will or living trust. It is a letter to clarify your wishes and send your everlasting love to the special people in your life. Your letter can be as long or as short as you prefer, but usually it includes the bullet points below. By the way, be sure to tell your friends and family that you've written the letter. Keep a copy with your will and important papers. You can revise the letter at any time, so be sure to date and sign each letter because the latest date will prevail.

- **Funeral wishes:** Are you having a funeral or a celebration? I'm serious. Let your family know your wishes for the spirit of the event. This gives them permission to honor you as you wish. Here is a chance to make decisions easier for them by deciding in advance **where** the funeral will take place and where you want to be buried, **who** will officiate and who will be the pallbearers, **how** the service will be delivered (with songs, live music, testimonials, eulogy), **when** it will take place if you have a preference of a time of day, **what** you want written in your obituary and even **why** some of these requests are important to you.
- **Personal items:** Now is the time to assign personal items such as jewelry, golf clubs, artwork or other items that have a sentimental value to the specific friend or family member you wish to own them.
- **Financial items:** Even though you may have all of your financial information in one location, this is a good place to list all of your bank accounts, pension plans, insurances; the names and contact numbers for your attorney, insurance agent, banker and retirement planner; the location of your Social Security card, insurance policies, birth certifi-

cate, titles and deeds, and marriage certificates; and any bills or credit card information.

- **Goodbyes:** You may use this occasion to say your final goodbyes and anything that you want to leave as a lasting memory. We rarely depart this world in a Hollywood ending, gazing into the eyes of those we love. Just to be safe, put your "I love you" in your letter of instruction.

# Wills and Trusts

I purposely saved the two biggest estate-planning tools for last. I'd like to say that wills and trusts are perfect tools. But, they're not. Each has its own set of advantages and disadvantages.

- **Will:** A legal document that allows you to decide how your estate will be managed and distributed after your death.
- **Living trust:** A legal document that allows you to place your home, investments and other assets into a trust where they will be administered for your benefit while you are alive and transferred to your beneficiaries upon your death. Generally, living trusts are used by people with assets exceeding $100,000 as a means to avoid probate and to reduce estate and gift taxes.

Wills and trusts are designed to solve the same problem, that of distributing your estate according to your wishes. However, there are many types of trusts, which vary from state to state, so be sure to consult the attorney on your retirement planning team.

## Pros and Cons of Wills

Wills cost less to set up than trusts and are fairly simple documents. You can retain full ownership of your property until the day that you die, and creditors have a deadline for any claims against your estate. You can also designate a guardian for your minor children.

On the other hand, wills must go to probate. We feel you can just cross out the word "Will" and write in "Dear Judge"! This takes time and can be costly. It also robs you of privacy because your will becomes public record upon probate. It can also be difficult to designate a replacement executor if your named executor becomes incapable.

## Pros and Cons of Living Trusts

A living trust avoids probate in most states, thereby protecting your privacy. The distribution of your estate does not become a matter of public record. It also protects your pocketbook because probate costs can be expensive. You can't name a guardian for your minor children in a living trust, but you can designate someone to manage the property that your minor children inherit. You would need a supplemental will to name a guardian. Living trust may offer tax benefits. You would need to consult with the attorney who is part of your retirement planning team.

There are some disadvantages to living trusts. It costs more to set up a living trust than a will. Because assets are transferred into the trust, it requires considerably more legal paperwork. Creditors filing claims against your estate do not have a deadline. Additionally, it is very difficult to refinance property after it has been transferred into a living trust.

I think it's apparent that I did not give you enough information to make a decision about your estate planning. No matter how much I write here, it will never be enough, because this is a decision that has to take into account your personal goals, assets, risk tolerances and preferences. Because the consequences of estate planning are so far-reaching, this is the time to call your whole retirement planning team together — your retirement planner, attorney and accountant — to create the plan that is a custom fit for your needs.

# IRA Blooper

From a tax standpoint, it is always best to name a person, not a trust, as beneficiary to your IRA. Take a look at two scenarios with a retiree we'll call Jack.

In the first scenario, Jack lists by name his two children, Bob and Beth, as primary beneficiaries and his four grandchildren by name as his secondary beneficiaries of his $400,000 IRA. Upon his demise, Jack's two children request that the funds be split. Bob decides that this is the perfect time to start up his new business and accepts a check for $200,000. When tax time rolls around, Bob finds out that, for income tax purposes, he has to add the $200,000 to his $70,000 per year salary for a total taxable income of $270,000. His tax rate jumps from 25 percent to 33 percent. Of the initial $200,000 inheritance, $66,000 goes to Uncle Sam, leaving Bob $134,000. That is certainly not what his father had in mind, nor is it what Bob expected.

Beth, on the other hand, had been regularly working with a retirement planning specialist. Before making any decisions, she talked to her planner. After hearing her choices and working out the various tax consequences, Beth decided to "stretch" her inherited IRA. Following the rules set out in Publication 590 in the IRS Codebook, Beth made sure to do a trustee-trustee transfer and renamed the IRA, which included the original owner's name, indicating that this was an inherited IRA. This action allowed Beth to leave most of the $200,000 to grow tax deferred. Beth was only required to take an annual RMD (required minimum distribution) based on her age, thereby "stretching" the benefits over her lifetime. For Beth, her RMD amounted to $5,500. Incidentally, Beth also earned $70,000 per year and the additional taxable income didn't change her tax bracket. She paid Uncle Sam $1,375 in taxes on her RMD. Beth retained $198,625 of her father's gift to her. (She still had $4,125 ($5,500 - $1,375), but it was in her savings account instead of the IRA.) Lastly, the $194,500 that remained in her stretch IRA grew by 5 percent, or $9,725. At the end of the year, Beth had an extra $4,125 in her savings account and $204,255 in her stretch IRA.

At this point, things look pretty good for Beth and not so good for Bob. But what would happen if Jack had listed his IRA in his living trust? His $400,000 IRA proceeds would be taxed at estate and trust rates. As of the writing of this book, the first $11,950 would have a base rate tax of $3,090. The remaining $396,910 would be taxed at 39.6 percent. That means that Uncle Sam would receive $160,266 ($396,910 x .396 = $157,176 plus the base tax $3,090 for a total $160,266). Then, Beth and Bob would split the balance ($400,000 - 160,266 tax

= \$239,734 to be split) and each receive a check for \$119,867. As crazy as it sounds, Uncle Sam actually received more of an inheritance from Jack than his own two children.

If this doesn't teach us anything else, we ought to learn that it pays to ask for professional help when setting up our estate plan and before we make any major financial decisions. Personally, I assisted a client who recently lost her father, a prominent and intelligent educator. He listed his estate as his beneficiary on his 401(k), and because of that, the funds went to the creditors instead of his daughter. Normally, qualified funds don't go to creditors unless we make a fatal estate planning mistake such as that. Because he didn't seek counsel and just wrote a default on a form, it cost his family a quarter of a million dollars.

I could now proceed to write the exact wording that is necessary to create a "stretch" IRA or even the jargon to create an "online" will or trust. But if I did that, I'd be doing you a huge disservice. It might give some people a false confidence that they could objectively create all of their legal documents without consulting a professional. In this book, and specifically in this chapter, I've purposely included real-life disasters to demonstrate the unintended consequences of "self-guided" retirement planning. You owe it to yourself to add in the human factor by meeting face-to-face with a retirement planner.

Personally, I don't know of anyone who has ever attended one of my seminars or met with me for a free consultation in my office and has left not knowing at least one way to improve their retirement or estate plan.

---

# S.H.I.E.L.D.

Did you happen to notice the acronym S.H.I.E.L.D. on the banner at the bottom of the shield?

**S=Safety, H=Health, I=Income, E=Estate, L=Legacy and D=Diversity = S.H.I.E.L.D.**

By properly employing insurance, we make sure that your **safety** and **health** are protected throughout your retirement.

Savings, annuities, Social Security, pension plans and other investments provide you with retirement **income**, some guaranteed to last your lifetime.

Our five tools — power of attorney, will and/or living trust, health care directive, beneficiary deed and letter of instruction protect your **estate.**

Once protected, we use the tools of beneficiaries, TODs, PODs, insurance, wills and/or living trusts to pass on your **legacy** as you intend.

We reinforce your retirement plan by employing the right types of **diversity** to keep your plan balanced and healthy.

This strong shield of protection can help give you the confidence of knowing your retirement plan is well constructed and protected.

# ABOUT THE AUTHOR

Alan E. Becker, president and CEO of Retirement Solutions Group and RSG Investments, lives in Olathe, Kansas, a fast-growing community about 20 miles southwest of Kansas City. Olathe placed No. 11 on CNN and Money magazine's "100 Best Cities to Live in the Nation" list, and Alan wholeheartedly agrees with that assessment. It is a town that he says agrees with his Midwestern values and is, in his words, "the perfect place to live and raise my family."

"This is my story. One of anguish and triumph as life can throw us all curve balls. It's not about predicting what may come at you — but it's about being prepared for what could happen. This is why I do what I do," states Alan.

Alan was born in Shreveport, Louisiana, in 1973. His father, Robert Becker, was a career Air Force member. To say that the family moved around a lot during his youth is an understatement. In fact, Alan narrowly missed being born on the Pacific island of Okinawa, where his father was stationed in the early 1970s.

"I was made in Japan and born in the USA," Alan jokes. He spent his early childhood in Warner Robbins, Georgia; lived in Oscoda, Michigan until the age of 9; and also moved to Austin, Texas, before the family finally settled down in Kansas, where Alan's mother, Fran, was born and raised. This is where Alan spent his teen years.

"I have worked at something for as long as I can remember," Alan says. "Mowing lawns, washing cars and I even remember selling candy bars door-to-door when we lived in Texas."

Growing up, Alan was one of those people who loved learning but hated school.

"I will never forget one teacher in particular who took an interest in me." Alan remembers, "Mrs. Davis said, 'You don't like school because you're bored. What if we double up your classes and get you out at the end of semester?'" Alan took the offer. He graduated from high school at age 17. Eager to learn even more, Alan joined the United States Navy and saw the world, literally.

"Curiosity took over when I stuck my head inside the Navy recruiting office," Alan said. "I knew I would finish my education someday, but at 17, I was just itching for adventure. I soon found myself aboard a huge Navy ship, the

USS Ranger. My first job was cleaning berths as a ship's serviceman. Later, they taught me to cut hair and I became a barber."

Alan served mainly in the west Pacific. His ports of call included Hong Kong, Singapore, and Perth and Sydney, Australia. Alan completed two West-Pac deployments, each six months out at sea, including several months in the Persian Gulf. "Technically, I was in Operation Southern Watch," Alan says. "Operation Desert Storm was over and Operation Enduring Freedom hadn't started yet." After four years and eight months aboard two ships, his thirst for adventure slaked, Alan was free to pursue his education at Johnson County Community College in Overland Park, Kansas.

After college, Alan went to work as an insurance agent for American Income Life. After five years of 10-hour days each Monday through Saturday, he was ready for a change. Leaving was bittersweet, and Alan's state general agent told him he was the "most-decorated agent" they had ever seen. At this point in his career, Alan was running an office in St. Louis, when his mentor, Dan Stevens, called and asked him to join him at Bankers Life and Casualty Company. Alan took the opportunity to return to his roots in Kansas City, where he worked over the next five years. In 1999, his first year with Bankers Life and Casualty, he took home the "Division Agent of the Year" and the coveted "Rookie Agent of the Year" awards. At Bankers, Alan ranked in the Top 10 across the entire country.

Through life tribulations and the Conseco financial downfall, company decisions took a personal toll on Alan's family. Bankers dropped the health insurance for all of the agents, including Alan and his family. So, without health insurance, he was forced to seek other opportunities to protect his family. Penn Life arrived on the scene and presented him the opportunity to run his own branch in Kansas City, where they had just launched their new Medicare Advantage program.

Alan soon discovered that he was limited solely as an insurance agent. Alan was told by the executives at Penn Life that "he wasn't allowed to offer a product that a client needed, even though they had a contract with that carrier." Alan could not morally accept that answer because it was not in the best interest of his client. This incident was the best thing that could have happened. Due to company policies limiting his abilities, he decided to challenge himself and form his own company. With the help of many mentors and other trusted associates, he formed KC Senior Solutions Retirement Group, which eventually morphed into Retirement Solutions Group, Inc. in 2010. Alan later passed his Series 65 exam and became an Investment Advisor Representative. RSG and RSG Investments has grown into a full-service comprehensive financial advisory firm specializing in the retirement realm of financial planning.

Alan describes himself as a people person and not a paper pusher. "My passion lies not in selling insurance or investments, but using them to solve problems," he states.

Alan hosts "Retire Right Radio," a Kansas City radio program that airs Saturday and Sunday mornings on several different stations across the metro area. The show reaches thousands of people and helps educate them about the importance of retirement and estate planning. Alan has also written several articles that have been published in various financial and business journals.

Community involvement and charitable causes are always on the forefront of Alan's mind. Bikers for Babies, community blood drives and the Make-A-Wish Foundation are just a few examples of how Alan gives back to his community. His hobbies include spending time with his family camping, participating in fund raisers that benefit fellow veterans and traveling, when time permits.

# ACKNOWLEDGMENTS

This book has been carefully crafted with love and passion for what I have been blessed to do every day. I'm in the **tomorrow business**! I help protect families' "happily-ever-afters." I truly don't feel I have a job and have not gone to *work* in years. I have a life choice and a passion that drives me to help people. What a wonderful world.

None of this would have been possible if it wasn't for the dedication and shared passion of my RSG family and team. They've endured countless late-night seminars, out-of-town business trips and educational activities — compounded with late-night and emergency client visits. It's always been a priority to make the team available to our baby boomers when they need us. The growth we have had since I formed my planning firm has been more than I could have ever imagined.

Surrounding myself with driven, intelligent and caring individuals has been my most successful business decision. I know without my team, RSG would not be what it is today. There are moments when I wonder if I will ever be able to say "thank you" enough to some, and some days I wonder, "Was it all worth it?" The answer to this question is an easy one — when a widow comes in and gives you a hug or her shoulders relax back as a sigh of relief passes over her, I can easily tell myself "Yes, I'm doing what God wants me to do as his steward." All the doubts go away. To all who have worked with me in the past, or will in the future, I thank you for making this all possible.

Made in the USA
San Bernardino, CA
19 April 2017